GIRLS' NIGHT

Over 1,000 Drinks for Going Out, Staying In, and Having Fun!

Jaclyn Wilson Foley

SOURCEBOOKS, INC.
NAPERVILLE, ILLINOIS

Published by Sourcebooks, Inc.
P.O. Box 4410, Naperville, Illinois   60567-4410
(630) 961-3900
FAX: (630) 961-2168
www.sourcebooks.com

Originally published in 2003

Library of Congress Cataloging-in-Publication Data
Foley, Jaclyn.
  Girls' night : over 1,000 drinks for going out, staying in and having fun! /
Jaclyn Foley.
     p. cm.
  1. Cocktails. 2. Women—Alcohol use. I. Title.

TX951.F58 2007
641.8'74—dc22
                                            2006016344

Printed and bound in the United States of America.
CH   13 12 11 10

DEDICATION

To my son Ryan Peter Foley and my husband
Raymond Peter Foley, who have both con-
tributed to this book and most importantly to
my happiness.

And to the 150,000-plus readers and follow-
ers of *Bartender* magazine who sent us recipes,
ideas, and inspiration that helped to contribute
to the success of *Girls' Night*.

CONTENTS

ACKNOWLEDGMENTS

I'd like to thank my sponsors for their contribution to *Girls' Night*.

Jim Beam Brands Worldwide, Inc. with special thanks to Mike Donohoe, Kathleen DiBenedetto, Heather Mitchell, and Chris Gretchko for Vox vodka, Knob Creek bourbon, and DeKuyper cordials.

Vox Vodka: Vox vodka is a pristine, ultra-premium spirit imported from the Netherlands and created for a chilled cocktail glass. Vox is a spirit of exceptional smoothness, unsurpassed clarity and a cool finish. Vox is distilled from 100 percent wheat, chosen for its mildness and ability to give the vodka a remarkable smoothness. The clarity of Vox is attained by using demineralized water produced through a careful process of reverse osmosis to remove all traces of color and odor. Vox is then distilled five times, at a very high proof, to remove any elements that could taint the final product.

Knob Creek: Handcrafted in limited quantities using time-honored recipes, aged a full nine years, and hand-bottled at an honest 100 proof, Knob Creek bourbon has established itself as an exceptional whiskey. Daring to set new standards, Knob Creek even dares to look entirely different, housed in a unique flask-shaped bottle.

DeKuyper Cordials: For more than three hundred years, DeKuyper has been the brand to turn to for fresh and original liqueurs. DeKuyper has survived this ever-changing market by combining its rich traditional expertise with modern innovations and a healthy dash of imagination. From the punch of Original Peachtree schnapps or the fiery bite of Hot Damn! to the mouthwatering tang of Pucker sour apple schnapps, John DeKuyper & Son has created a magical array of exciting flavors and colors.

JSH&A Public Relations with special thanks to Laura Dihel, Kate McCutcheon, and Jim Kokoris.

Future Brands LLC with special thanks to Alan Mervish.

Bacardi USA, Inc. with special thanks to Lydia Holland, Celio Romanach, Joy Suchlicki, Mark Dean, Ria Campbell, Sumindi Peiris, Michael

Curry, Christine Moll, Monica Garaitonandia, John Gomez, Joe Metevier, and Gonzalo de la Pezuela for Bacardi rums, Bombay Sapphire gin, Disaronno amaretto, Dewar's scotch, Martini & Rossi vermouths, and Drambuie.

Bacardi Rum: How is it that Bacardi rum is the most popular spirit in the world today? Unique taste. Outstanding quality. Unequaled mixability. And a natural complement to so many great foods. It's a rum as rich in taste as in its own history. Because the rum bares a proud family name, to this day the quality of Bacardi rum has never been allowed to falter. Bacardi rum is one of America's favorite drinks and is also one of the most mixable. It can be used with all mixes and juices and is a great product to use when creating your own special drink.

Bombay Gin/Bombay Sapphire Gin: The recipe for Bombay gin dates back to 1761, and the botanicals—including coriander, lemon peel, angelica, licorice, anise, juniper, almonds, and cassia bark—are imported from around the world. The spirit used in Bombay's production comes from a distillery in Ayrshire, Scotland, and the soft, pure water is drawn from the Welsh Hills. Bombay owes its growing success to a uniquely slow and unhurried distillation process that ensures the consistently high standard of Bombay gin.

Unlike other gins, which boil their botanicals with the spirit, the Bombay Sapphire spirit is distilled alone. To achieve the unique flavor of Bombay Sapphire, the spirit passes through the botanicals in vapor form. This allows each delicate aroma to be fully absorbed. The result is Bombay Sapphire gin, a complex yet subtle taste sensation.

Disaronno Amaretto: Disaronno is made using only the highest quality ingredients like absolute alcohol, burnt sugar, and the pure essence of seventeen selected herbs and fruits soaked in apricot kernel oil. This special recipe hasn't changed since 1525.

Dewar's White Label: Dewar's White Label is a sophisticated blended scotch whisky that's honeyed and spicy, yet light and smoky. Taste the smoothness that could only come from forty of Scotland's finest single malts and grain whiskies and over 150 years of bold, Dewar's Scottish tradition.

Martini & Rossi Vermouths: In 1863, three partners joined together to found a company that today is the market leader in the vermouth industry. They took over an established eighteenth-century firm that had been producing vermouth in Torino, Italy, and by the end of the year, were exporting the first Martini vermouth for sale in the United States. Martini & Rossi vermouth is a true aperitif—that is, a wine incorporating aromatic substances and bitter plants; it is differentiated from other aromatized wines by the presence of bitter plants which stimulate digestive juices. Martini & Rossi's success is based upon its reputation as the finest vermouth in the world—one well earned and carefully preserved.

Drambuie: From the Gaelic meaning "the drink that satisfies," Drambuie is a rich combination of fine aged scotch whiskies, heather honey, and the secret ingredients of the original recipe.

Rèmy Amerique with special thanks to Jane Scott and Susan Mitchell for Cointreau.

Cointreau: Cointreau has been a worldwide legend since its creation in 1849. The innovation of the Cointreau family over 150 years has made Cointreau one of the world's most famous and successful liqueurs. It is the authentic choice of many top bartenders, and you will always find Cointreau in the smartest and most fashionable bars. The warm amber colored bottle with its rounded shoulders and red ribbon has remained virtually the same for 150 years, yet has retained its impact and appeal.

Diageo with special thanks to Debbie Greene for Jose Cuervo tequila.

Jose Cuervo: For over two hundred years, the Jose Cuervo family has produced the finest tequila in the world. This untamed spirit, steeped in legend and mystique, can trace its origins back as far as the 1770s. An entire lifetime dedicated to the pursuit of tradition and heritage allows Jose Cuervo to reign supreme. Jose Cuervo Especial has established the "gold standard" by becoming the number one tequila in the world.

Schieffelin & Somerset with special thanks to Christy Frank for Hennessy cognac.

Hennessy Cognac: In 1765, Richard Hennessy laid the foundation of a priceless collection made up of his most exceptional eaux de vie. For more than seven generations, the same family of Cellar Masters has watched over Hennessy's stocks. Today, it is Yann Fillious who continues the family tradition, often using eaux de vie set aside by his grandfather in the cognacs he creates for Hennessy. This commitment to tradition and continuity is the essence of what sets Hennessy V.S, V.S.O.P. Privilege, X.O, Private Reserve, Paradis Extra, and Richard Hennessy cognacs apart from the crowd.

Charles Jacquin, et Cie., Inc. with special thanks to Robert Cooper and Kevin O'Brien for Chambord.

Chambord: Chambord is made in small batches to ensure that only the ripest fruits are used. Chambord cultivates the finest framboises noires (small black raspberries) that are the essence of the liqueur. Chambord is a world-class liqueur enjoyed by the world's most discriminating tastes, and the same family has owned and produced Chambord for generations. Each successive son has passed down a passion for quality that has remained unchanged from the very beginning.

C&C International with special thanks to Alan B. Lewis for Carolans Irish cream, Irish Mist liqueur, and Tullamore Dew Irish whiskey.

Carolans: Carolans is produced in Clonmel in County Tipperary. The place name is derived from the Irish words "Clauin Meala," which means "Vale of Honey." This is very appropriate for Carolans, which includes honey in the recipe. All Irish cream liqueurs combine cream, Irish whiskey, spirits, and flavors for their taste, but there the similarities end. The technological process used in making Carolans is unique, ensuring a rich, creamy taste and superior shelf life. Also, the flavors are different in Carolans; in particular, the use of honey.

Irish Mist: Imagine the wonderful taste of aged Irish whiskey, blended with honey, herbs, and other spirits to a perfect smoothness. Now visualize that golden liqueur in a sleek bottle with gracefully swirling motif and jewel-like label, perfectly representing the contemporary Ireland of the twenty-first century.

That's Irish Mist—a smart, versatile drink for today's generation with years of quality and history behind it. Enjoy it on its own, with ice, mixed into a memorable cocktail, or as the vital ingredient in an Ultimate Irish Coffee.

Tullamore Dew. One of Ireland's finest and most widely distributed whiskeys, Tullamore Dew was first distilled in 1829 in the small town of Tullamore in County Offaly in the heart of Ireland. The name derives from the initials of an early owner, Daniel E. Williams—DEW. Tullamore Dew is a favorite among Irish whiskeys for its distinctive, accessible taste, enjoyed on its own, over ice, or with a little water. Connoisseurs describe Tullamore Dew as "subtle, smooth, and with a pleasant maltiness combined with charred wood undertones and the natural flavor of golden barley."

The Cherry Marketing Institute with special thanks to Cheryl Kroupa for the fabulous maraschino cherry.

INTRODUCTION

Welcome!

Bartending is an art. It's the art of making cocktails and mixing with people. It's the art of hospitality and creativity. It's the art of listening and understanding. It's the art of sales and service. It's fashion. It's society and sensibility. It's patience and pouring.

When tending bar, you learn a tremendous amount about people, both good and could do without! In my case, 99 percent good and only 1 percent could do without. *Girls' Night* is my look at bartending and cocktails from a woman's viewpoint. I do believe in creativity for all—get crazy, get creative, and pull out all the stops. Let's decorate, use fun glassware, great garnishes, and have fabulous times!

It's called *bartending* and we are bartenders, not barmaids, goddesses, bargirls, Ms. mixologists, or Master mixologists. We are good, hardworking, and creative bartenders.

In the selection of brands for *Girls' Night*, I have chosen top-of-the-line products. Always use the best ingredients to insure the best tasting cocktails. Using the best makes the best! There are no substitutions.

The bar business has been my life for the last twenty-two years. I now have the opportunity to share with you some tips, clues, and cocktails.

Please always remember, never drink to excess. Moderation is the key in all things. Use good judgment not only for yourself, but when serving guests. Drinking and driving do not mix at all, ever! The cocktails in *Girls' Night* are for your pleasure in moderation. Enjoy.

CALORIES & CARBOHYDRATES

	Calories	Carbohydrates
Ale	72	
Beer (12 oz. bottle or can)	144	1 1.7
Light Beer	110	6.9
Bourbon		
80 proof, distilled	65	trace
86 proof, distilled	70	trace
90 proof, distilled	74	trace
94 proof, distilled	77	trace
100 proof, distilled	83	trace
Brandy		
80 proof, distilled	65	trace
86 proof, distilled	70	trace
90 proof, distilled	74	trace
94 proof, distilled	77	trace
100 proof, distilled	83	trace
Champagne		
Brut (4 fl. oz.)	92	2.1
Extra Dry	97	2.1

Pink	98	3.7

Coffee Liqueur

53 proof	117	16.3
63 proof	107	11.2

Crème de Menthe, 72 proof .... 125 .... 14.0

Gin

80 proof (1 oz.)	65	0.0
86 proof (1 oz.)	70	0.0
90 proof (1 oz.)	74	0.0
94 proof (1 oz.)	77	0.0
100 proof (1 oz.)	83	0.0

Rum

80 proof (1 oz.)	65	0.0
86 proof (1 oz.)	70	0.0
90 proof (1 oz.)	74	0.0
94 proof (1 oz.)	77	0.0
100 proof (1 oz.)	83	0.0

Scotch

80 proof, distilled	65	trace
86 proof, distilled	70	trace
90 proof, distilled	74	trace
94 proof, distilled	77	trace
100 proof, distilled	83	trace

Tequila

80 proof, distilled	64	0.0
86 proof, distilled	69	0.0
90 proof, distilled	73	0.0
94 proof, distilled	76	0.0
100 proof, distilled	82	0.0

Vodka

80 proof (1 oz.)	65	0.0
86 proof (1 oz.)	70	0.0
90 proof (1 oz.)	74	0.0
94 proof (1 oz.)	77	0.0
100 proof (1 oz.)	83	0.0

Whiskey

80 proof (1 oz.)	65	0.0
86 proof (1 oz.)	70	0.0
90 proof (1 oz.)	74	0.0
94 proof (1 oz.)	77	0.0
100 proof (1 oz.)	83	0.0

Wine

Aperitif (1 oz.)	41	2.3
Port (1 oz.)	41	2.3
Sherry (1 oz.)	41	2.3
White or Red Table (1 oz.)	29	1.2

Nonalcoholic

Club Soda (1 oz.) ....0 ....0.0

Cola (1 oz.) ....12 ....3.1

Cream Soda (1 oz.) ....13 ....3.4

Fruit-Flavored Soda (1 oz.) ....13 ....3.7

Ginger Ale (1 oz.) ....9 ....2.4

Root Beer (1 oz.) ....13 ....3.2

Tonic Water (1 oz.) ....9 ....2.4

DRESSING UP THE DRINK—GARNISHES

You drink with your eyes, and the prettier you can make a drink, the more appealing it is. You can have a great tasting drink, but if it does not look good then no one will want to taste it. In this case, you do judge a book by its cover and a drink by its garnish. Below are some ideas for garnishes and a simple lesson on cutting shapes of some basic fruits and vegetables. But remember: use your imagination and personality; you can get wild with garnishes.

Always make sure your garnishes are fresh and clean.

Types of Cut

Slice: A thinly cut portion, with a bit of peel on top, or half a wheel

Twist: Made by using a paring knife to cut away a thin portion of peel, which will naturally twist

Wedge: A triangular cut portion of the fruit or veggie

Wheel: A whole slice; the fruit or veggie from peel to peel

Types of Garnish

Apples, Apricots, Peaches, and Plums: They look best sliced. Peaches in particular make a great champagne garnish.

Bananas: Slices or wheels. Make sure the bananas are not too ripe.

Celery: Whole stalk with flower

Chocolate Sticks: They make a great stirrer and garnish in one. (And I know these are available at Bloomingdale's.)

Cinnamon Sticks: Great for hot drinks.

Cloves: Add them whole to hot drinks.

Cocktail Onions: Whole onions are usually used in a Gibson Cocktail.

Coffee Beans: Three beans are usually dropped into sambuca, sometimes flamed. I do not recommend flaming.

Cucumber: A slice or a twist makes a very nice decoration.

Flowers: Rose pedals, small baby orchids, or any other flower look great in most tall cocktails and add a great visual effect.

Fresh Herbs: Mint is the most popular, but you can use cilantro, basil, rosemary, and thyme. Many herbs work well in Bloody Marys and of course mint is commonly known as being in the Mint Julep or Mojito. But remember, mint can be used in a garnish as you see fit. It looks nice and it smells great. Use your imagination!

Lemons: Twist, slices, wheels, and wedges

Limes: Twist, slices, wheels, and wedges

Maraschino Cherries: The fun fruit. It looks good, tastes good, and adds value to any drink or desert. The maraschino originates from an Italian liqueur that used the local "Marasca" cherry as its base. Originally brought to the United States in the 1890s from regions of Yugoslavia and Italy, by 1920 the American maraschino had replaced the foreign versions. American producers used a domestic sweet cherry called the Royal Anne cherry and eliminated the use of liquor in the processing, substituting it with almond oil.

The modern day maraschino is primarily grown in Oregon, Washington, and Michigan and is characterized by its bright, uniform color and cherry fruit flavor with just a mere hint of almond.

Olives: Whole black and green, both can be stuffed with almonds, anchovies, blue cheese, or pimentos

Oranges: Twist, slices, wheels, and wedges

Pineapples: Wedges, also use the whole pineapple as a serving container

Pink Grapefruit: Though bitter, large grapefruit slices or wheels can add a burst of flavor.

Raspberries: Whole or muddled

Salt: Table salt, sea salt, and kosher salt are used to coat the rim of the glass and are mostly for Margaritas or a Salty Dog. You can also add half sugar to the salt, which makes for an interesting taste. Colored salts are also available and fun.

Sugar: Can be used to coat drinks. Cubes can be used in champagne drinks, and there are colored sugars available as well.

Strawberries: Sliced and hung on the side of the glass

"Toys": Non-edible plastic mermaids, Barrel of Monkeys, baby ducks, umbrellas, fancy straws and stirrers, and little boats add a fun element to a drink. Make sure they are small enough to fit in the drink and large enough so you can't swallow them. Remember these "toys" are not for children under twenty-one.

CUTTING FRUIT

Different kinds of fruit are used to garnish different kinds of drinks. Remember to wash all fruit and vegetables before cutting.

Lemon Twist: 1) Cut off both ends. 2) Using a sharp knife or spoon, insert between rind and meat, carefully separating. 3) Cut skin into 1/4 inch strips.

Celery: 1) Cut off bottom of celery. You may cut off top also. 2) If leaf is fresh, you may use this as garnish. 3) Cut celery stalk in half.

Oranges: 1) Cut oranges in half. 2) Slice orange in half. 3) Half moon cut.

Limes: 1) Cut ends of lime. 2) Slice lime into half. 3) Cut in half moons.

Wedges (Lemon/Limes): 1) Slice lime in half. 2) Cut halves flat down and half again. 3) Cut to 1/4 inch to 1/2 inch wedges.

Pineapple: 1) Cut off top and bottom. 2) Cut pineapple in half. 3) Cut in half again. 4) Cut 1/2 inch slices. 5) Cut wedges.

MIXERS & ENHANCERS

Here's a great way to add creativity and sparkle to a drink: by adding a great mix or enhancer. Changing the color, texture, and taste of the alcohol with a juice or other product can make it memorable. Mixers and enhancers should also be on hand for people who do not drink alcohol. (Be sure to check the section on nonalcoholic drinks.)

When using juices, make sure you check the expiration date and use the liquid quickly after opening, because there is nothing worse than a juice that has gone bad. Don't let your enhancer be a distracter.

Fruit Juice

Apple Juice: Bottled apple juice is the best. Check dates.

Clamato Juice: A mixture of clam and tomato juice.

Cranberry Juice Cocktail: Excellent bottled.

Grapefruit Juice: Fresh is best, but like orange

juice, some carton and frozen varieties can do the job.

Lime Juice: If you cannot get fresh squeezed I highly recommend Rose's lime juice.

Orange Juice: Fresh squeezed is the best but there are great frozen and carton varieties available.

Pineapple Juice: Bottled is best.

Tomato Juice: Bottled juice is best. For Bloody Marys try using V-8.

Other Mixers

Try your local grocery store for a variety of new and mixed juice drinks like cranapple. Ocean Spray has a ton of new juice mixes, go out and try some, have fun, and experiment. You may surprise yourself.

SODA: cola or diet cola, Dr. Pepper, ginger ale, lemon-lime soda, root beer, seltzer water or club soda, tonic water

*Check your local store; there are many region-specific sodas that can add zest to a drink.

OTHER MIXERS:

beef bullion, cappuccino, clam juice, Coco Lopez cream of coconut, coffee, espresso, half-and-half, heavy cream, honey, ice cream, lemon juice or lemon mix, and tea.

ENHANCERS:

Angostura Bitters

Chocolate Syrup: A good quality chocolate syrup can make a great chocolate martini and add flavor to any ice cream drink.

Egg Whites: Not recommended for use due to food safety reasons.

Falernum Syrup: A rum-based syrup from Barbados with a refined infusion of lime laced with fine cane syrup and "botanicals" including almonds and cloves.

Fruit Syrups: There are many available such as strawberry, raspberry, and other berries. For more information on the syrups available contact Monin (www.monin.com).

Horseradish

Orgeat Syrup: Flavored with almonds and

orange-flavored water.

Peychauds Bitters: Available from the Sazerac Company (www.sazerac.com/bitters.html).

Rose's Grenadine
Rose's Lime Juice
Worcestershire Sauce

POUSSE-CAFÉ

Pousse-Café is French for "after coffee." They are layered specialty drinks. By adding the ingredients in order of their specific gravity they will remain separate and the result is a colorful rainbow effect. I have included two sample recipes as well as a specific gravity chart and a color-layering guide. Use these to create your very own pousse-cafés!

ANGEL'S KISS

1 oz. DeKuyper dark crème de cacao

Top with cream.

TRAFFIC LIGHT

1/3 DeKuyper green crème de menthe
1/3 Carolans Irish cream
1/3 Cointreau

Specific Density Chart

Product	Proof	Density
DeKuyper Coffee Liqueur	53	1.1389
DeKuyper Almond Liqueur	56	1.1294
DeKuyper Butterscotch Schnapps	30	1.1225
DeKuyper Crème de Cassis	40	1.1211
DeKuyper Dark Crème de Cacao	54	1.1141
DeKuyper Pucker Sour Apple Schnapps	30	1.0944
DeKuyper Pucker Cheri-Beri	30	1.0937
DeKuyper Coconut Amaretto	48	1.0925
DeKuyper Anisette Liqueur	60	1.0921
DeKuyper Green Crème de Menthe	60	1.0885
DeKuyper Pucker Grape Schnapps	30	1.0864
DeKuyper Crantasia Schnapps	30	1.0863
DeKuyper Blueberry Schnapps	30	1.0863
Disaronno Amaretto	56	1.085
DeKuyper Apple Schnapps	48	1.0844
DeKuyper Banana	56	1.0822
Benedictine	80	1.0725
DeKuyper Blue Curacao	54	1.0704
DeKuyper Hazelnut Liqueur	56	1.0685
Galliano	60	1.065
DeKuyper Cinnamon Schnapps	60	1.0632
DeKuyper Blackberry Brandy	70	1.0552

DeKuyper Coffee Brandy	70	1.0543
DeKuyper Apricot Brandy	70	1.0437
DeKuyper Cactus Juice Schnapps	30	1.0430
DeKuyper Cherry Brandy	70	1.0392
Cointreau	80	1.0385
B & B	80	1.0245
DeKuyper Ginger Brandy	70	1.0060
Southern Comfort	80	09933

Layering Guide by Color

Product	Color
Grenadine	Red
DeKuyper Crème de Cassis	Red
DeKuyper Crème de Cacao	Brown
DeKuyper Coffee Liqueur	Brown
DeKuyper Peach Schnapps	Clear
DeKuyper Crème de Banana	Yellow
DeKuyper Anisette	Clear
DeKuyper Crème de Menthe	Green
DeKuyper Crème de Menthe	Clear
DeKuyper Melon	Green
DeKuyper Cherry Brandy	Red
DeKuyper Apricot Brandy	Gold
Galliano	Yellow

Disaronno Amaretto ....Tawny

Benedictine ....Gold

DeKuyper Peppermint Schnapps ....Clear

DeKuyper Spearmint Schnapps ....Clear

Irish Mist ....Gold

Cointreau ....Clear

DeKuyper Sloe Gin ....Red

B & B ....Gold

Chambord ....Purple

Drambuie ....Gold

Southern Comfort ....Gold

GLASSWARE

Today, about 40 percent of all cocktails are served in a martini glass. Can you serve a martini in a wine glass? Sure, serving cocktails in different types of glasses will not change the taste of the drink, just the serving glass. But a beer glass should always be used to serve beer, and a cream drink glass should be washed at least twice. Champagne should always be served in a champagne glass or flute. But also remember that glassware can add flare to a drink, so be creative. The following is a list of some common glassware that can bring vitality to your concoctions:

Brandy Snifters: Smaller sizes of the glasses, which come in sizes ranging from 5 1/2 to 22 ounces, are prefect for serving cognac, liqueurs, and premium whiskeys. The larger sizes provide enough space for a noseful of aroma, and the small stems on large bowls allow a cupped hand to warm the liquid.

Champagne Glass: A narrow version of the standard wine glass has a tapered bowl to prevent those tiny bubbles from escaping and is usually never more than half-filled. Also preferable for any sparkling liquid, including ciders.

Cocktail or Martini Glass: Perfect for martinis and manhattans. Remember that the stem is not just for show: it keeps hands from warming the drink. Available in 3 to 6 ounce sizes.

Collins Glass: The fraternal twin brother of the highball is often frosted and a tad taller, which adds a tropical look to many fruity drinks.

Coolers: These large capacity tumblers are taller and hold a lot of ice for larger concoctions. They have become popular as of late for nonalcoholic and extra volume highballs.

Highball Glass: Extremely versatile glass available in many sizes and used for almost any drink. Usually clear and tall, the most popular sizes range from 8 to 12 ounces.

Hurricane Glass: Tropical fruit drinks and Bloody Marys are perfectly suited for these 16 to 23 ounce tall, curved glasses.

Red Wine Glass: The wine glass with the slightly larger bowl which allows the red vintages to breathe but keeps the aroma trapped.

Rocks Glasses: These "old-fashioned" glasses hold from 6 to 10 ounces and are used for on-the-rocks presentations. Double rocks will run between 12 and 15 ounces.

Sherry Glass: Small 2 to 3 1/2 ounce stemmed glasses are perfect for sherry, port, and aperitifs.

Shot Glass: The old standby can also be used as a measuring glass and is a must for every bar.

White Wine Glass: Smaller wine glasses are preferable, though sizes range from 5 to 10 ounces.

TYPES OF DRINKS

There are seven basic ways of preparing a drink; you can blend, build, shake, stir, mix, layer, or muddle. Within these ways of preparing, though, come many types of drinks, and here are a few interesting ones. First off, I will quickly go over some of the older types of drinks.

Aperitif: A light alcohol drink served before lunch or dinner, sometimes bitter.

Cobbler: A tall drink usually filled with crushed ice and garnished with fruit or mint.

Crusta: Served in a wine glass with a sugar-coated rim and the inside of the glass lined with a citrus rind.

Cups: A traditionally British category of wine-based drinks.

Daisy: An oversized cocktail sweetened with fruit syrup served over crushed ice.

Eggnog: A blend of milk or cream, beaten eggs, sugar, and liquor, usually rum, brandy, or whiskey and sometimes Sherry topped with nutmeg.

Flip: Cold, creamy drinks made with eggs, sugar, alcohol, and citrus juice.

Highball: A tall drink usually served with whiskey and ginger ale. The favorite drink of many drinkers' grandparents.

Grog: A rum-based drink made with fruit and sugar.

Julep: A tall sweet drink usually made with bourbon, water, sugar, crushed ice, and occasionally mint. The most popular Julep being, of course, the Kentucky Derby's famous Mint Julep.

Puff: Made with equal parts alcohol and milk topped with club soda.

Pousse-Café: A drink made of layers created by floating liqueur according to their density (see page 19 on Pousse-Café cocktails and the accompanying density chart).

Rickey: A cocktail made of alcohol (usually whisky, lime juice, and soda water).

Sling: A tall drink made with lemon juice, sugar, and topped with club soda.

Smash: A short Julep.

Toddy: Served hot, it's a mixture of alcohol, spices, and hot water.

The following are more recent and popular drinks:

Blended Drinks: Blender drinks consisting of ice, ice cream, and a variety of other ingredients blended to a smooth though thick consistency.

Cream: Any drink made with ice cream, heavy cream, half-and-half, or any of the famous bottled cream drinks.

Mist: Any type of alcoholic beverage served over crushed ice.

Mojita: A Cuban-born drink prepared with sugar, muddled mint leaves, fresh lime juice, rum, ice, soda water, and garnished with mint leaves.

Shooter: A straight shot of alcohol, also sometimes called serving a drink "neat."

Sours: Drinks made with lemon juice, sugar, and alcohol.

The next two types of drinks are new on the scene and sure to be filling the glasses of those in the know at a bar near you:

Stixx: Tall muddled cocktails using different sized muddlers from 6 inches to 12 inches. Now there are muddling herbs, fruits, spices, and a variety of ethnic and regional ingredients including beans, roots, and spices.

Toppers: Blended drinks with ice cream or crushed ice, the thicker the better, which is why these drinks are served with a spoon and a straw. They are made using cordials, flavored rums, flavored vodkas, blended fresh fruits, and tropical juices. They are topped with crushed candy, fruits, nuts, and just about anything you can eat with a spoon.

COCKTAIL RECIPES

A.C.C.

1/2 oz. amaretto (Disaronno)
1/2 oz. Carolans Irish cream
1/2 oz. Cointreau

Build.

A MIDSUMMER NIGHT'S DREAM

1 1/2 oz. Jose Cuervo Especial
2 1/2 oz. pineapple juice
1/2 oz. lemonade
1/2 oz. Rose's grenadine

A TINKER TALL

1 1/4 oz. Irish Mist
3 oz. ginger ale
3 oz. club soda

Combine ingredients with lots of ice in a tall glass.

A-BOMB

1/2 oz. Vox vodka
1/2 oz. DeKuyper coffee liqueur
1/2 oz. Carolans Irish cream
1/2 oz. Cointreau

Shake with ice, strain, and serve in a highball glass.

A-BOMB II

1/2 oz. Carolans Irish cream
1/2 oz. DeKuyper coffee liqueur
1/2 oz. Vox vodka

Shake with ice and strain. You can also serve this one in a rocks glass.

ACAPULCO COCKTAIL

1 oz. Jose Cuervo tequila
2 oz. champagne
1/2 oz. lime juice

Sugar to taste. Stir gently.

ACAPULCO GOLD

1 1/4 oz. Jose Cuervo Especial tequila
5/8 oz. Cointreau
1 oz. sweet & sour mix

Blend with ice.

AFTER 5

1 part Carolans Irish cream
1 part DeKuyper peppermint schnapps

Pour the ingredients in a shot glass.

AFTER 8

1/2 oz. Carolans Irish cream
1/2 oz. DeKuyper coffee liqueur
1/2 oz. DeKuyper green crème de menthe

Shake with ice. Strain into a shot glass.

AFTER DINNER MINT

1 1/2 oz. DeKuyper dark crème de cacao
1/2 oz. Carolans Irish cream
2 drops DeKuyper green crème de menthe

Layer liquors in the order they are given. Serve in a shooter glass.

AFTER FIVE

1 oz. Carolans Irish cream
1 oz. DeKuyper peppermint schnapps
1/2 oz. DeKuyper coffee liqueur

Shake with ice and strain into a shot glass.

ALABAMA SLAMMER

1 part Disaronno amaretto
1 part DeKuyper sloe gin
1 part Southern Comfort
splash sweet & sour mix

Shake with ice and strain into a shot glass.

ALAMO SPLASH

1 1/2 oz. Jose Cuervo gold tequila
1 oz. orange juice
1/2 oz. pineapple juice
splash lemon-lime soda

Mix well with cracked ice. Strain and serve.

ALARM CLOCK

1 oz. Drambuie
1/2 oz. Bacardi dark rum
1/2 oz. Knob Creek bourbon

Shake with ice and strain.

ALBUQUERQUE RÉAL

1 1/2 oz. Jose Cuervo Especial tequila
1/2 oz. sweet & sour mix
1/4 oz. cranberry juice
1/4 oz. Cointreau

Stir all but Cointreau in the glass. Float the Cointreau.
Serve in a cocktail glass.

ALEXANDER'S SISTER

1 1/2 oz. Hennessy cognac
1 oz. DeKuyper white crème de menthe
1 oz. heavy cream or ice cream

Shake or blend and pour into a chilled cocktail glass.

ALGONQUIN

2 oz. Knob Creek bourbon
1/2 oz. Martini & Rossi dry vermouth
1 oz. pineapple juice

Combine all ingredients in a shaker and shake. Strain into a chilled cocktail glass.

ALLEGHENY

1 3/4 oz. Knob Creek bourbon
1/2 oz. Martini & Rossi dry vermouth
1 1/2 tsp. DeKuyper blackberry brandy
1 1/2 tsp. lemon juice

Shake with ice and strain into a cocktail glass. Add a twist of lemon peel on top.

ALL THAT RAZZ

2 oz. Bacardi Razz
1 oz. DeKuyper Peachtree schnapps
splash cranberry juice
splash pineapple juice

Shake and serve on the rocks.

Patrick
Funky Buddha
Chicago, IL

ALLIANCE

1 oz. Bombay Sapphire gin
1 oz. Martini & Rossi dry vermouth
2 dashes aquavit

Shake with ice and strain into a rocks glass over ice.

ALMOND JOY

1 oz. Disaronno amaretto
1 oz. DeKuyper white crème de cacao
2 oz. light cream

Shake all ingredients with ice, strain into a cocktail glass, and serve.

ALMOND JOY SHOOTER

1 1/2 oz. Disaronno amaretto
1/2 oz. DeKuyper dark crème de cacao
1/2 oz. Vox vodka
1/2 oz. cream

Shake with ice. Strain and serve straight up in a shot glass.

ALMOND LEMONADE

1 1/4 oz. Vox vodka
1/4 oz. Disaronno amaretto
lemonade

Shake with ice and strain into a shot glass.

ALOHA

1 oz. Vox vodka
1/2 oz. DeKuyper apricot brandy
2 oz. pineapple juice

*Shake with ice and serve in tall glass. Garnish with a
pineapple wedge.*

AMARETTO CAFE

1 1/2 oz. Disaronno amaretto
hot black coffee

Stir. Top with whipped cream.

AMBROSIA

1 oz. Laird's applejack
1 oz. brandy
1/4 oz. Cointreau
1/4 oz. lemon juice
champagne

Shake the first four ingredients over ice and strain into a champagne flute. Fill with champagne.

AMERICAN BEAUTY

1 oz. Hennessy cognac
1 oz. orange juice
1/2 oz. Martini & Rossi dry vermouth
1/4 tsp. DeKuyper white crème de menthe
1 tsp. Rose's grenadine
1/2 oz. tawny port

Shake with ice and strain into a cocktail glass. Float port.

AMERICAN DREAM

1/2 oz. Disaronno amaretto
1/2 oz. DeKuyper dark crème de cacao
1/2 oz. DeKuyper hazelnut liqueur
1/2 oz. DeKuyper coffee liqueur

Shake with ice. Strain and serve straight up in a cocktail glass.

AMERICAN ROSE

1 1/2 oz. Hennessy cognac
1 tsp. Rose's grenadine
1/2 fresh peach, peeled and mashed
dash Pernod
champagne

Mix all ingredients, except champagne, with ice in a shaker or blender and pour into a chilled wine goblet. Fill with champagne.

AMERICANO

1 oz. Martini & Rossi Rosso vermouth
1 oz. Campari
club soda

Build with ice in a highball glass. Top with club soda and a twist of lemon.

ANGEL'S KISS

1 1/2 oz. lime or lemon juice
1/2 oz. orange juice
1/2 oz. Cointreau
soda water

Pour lime (or lemon juice), orange juice, and Cointreau into a tumbler full of ice. Fill with soda water.

ANGEL'S DELIGHT

1 part Rose's grenadine
1 part Cointreau
1 part DeKuyper sloe gin
1 part heavy cream

Layer this drink in the order listed. Start with grenadine on the bottom and finish with cream on top.

ANTI-FREEZE

1 1/2 oz. Vox vodka
1/2 oz. DeKuyper melon liqueur

Shake with ice, strain, and serve. You can also serve this one in a rocks glass.

APPARENT

1/4 oz. Bombay Sapphire gin
1/4 oz. DeKuyper light crème de cacao

Shake and serve over rocks.

APPLE BLOSSOM

3/4 oz. DeKuyper Pucker sour apple
3/4 oz. soda water

Serve on the rocks.

APPLE CRANBERRY SPRITZER

1 oz. DeKuyper Pucker sour apple
1/2 oz. Vox vodka
4 oz. lemon-lime soda
1 1/2 oz. cranberry juice

Serve on the rocks.

APPLE CRUSH

1 1/2 oz. DeKuyper Pucker sour apple
dash lime juice

Fill a glass with ice and club soda.

APPLE DAIQUIRI

1 oz. Bacardi rum
1/2 oz. DeKuyper Pucker sour apple
1 oz. sweet & sour mix
2 wedges, cored apple
1 oz. apple juice

Blend with ice and serve with an apple slice garnish.

APPLE FIZZ

1 oz. DeKuyper Pucker sour apple
1/2 oz. DeKuyper San Tropique
splash lemon-lime soda

Add ice and fill with sweet & sour mix.

APPLE JACK

3/4 oz. DeKuyper Pucker sour apple
3/4 oz. Knob Creek bourbon

Stir and serve over ice.

APPLEJACK STINGER

2 oz. Laird's applejack
1 oz. DeKuyper white crème de menthe

Shake well with ice and strain into a cocktail glass or over ice.

APPLE KIR

1 oz. Jose Cuervo gold tequila
1/2 oz. DeKuyper crème de cassis
1 oz. apple juice
1 tsp. fresh lemon juice

Mix in a rocks glass over ice. Garnish with a lemon wedge.

APPLE LEMONADE

1 lemon, squeezed
1 1/4 oz. DeKuyper Pucker sour apple
3/4 oz. Vox vodka
1/2 oz. sugar water
1 oz. sweet & sour mix

Top with lemon-lime soda, and garnish with lemon and an apple wedge.

APPLE MARGARITA

1 1/4 oz. DeKuyper Pucker sour apple
3/4 oz. Jose Cuervo tequila
3/4 oz. lime juice
2 oz. sweet & sour mix

Shake with ice and serve.

APPLE PIE

1/2 oz. DeKuyper Pucker sour apple
1/2 oz. DeKuyper Hot Damn! schnapps

Serve over ice.

APPLE PIE A LA MODE

1 oz. DeKuyper Pucker sour apple
1/2 oz. DeKuyper Hot Damn!
2 scoops vanilla ice cream
2 wedges, cored apple
2 dashes cinnamon powder
2 oz. apple juice

Blend with ice and serve. Garnish with an apple slice.

APPLE PIÑA COLADA

3/4 oz. Bacardi rum
3/4 oz. DeKuyper Pucker sour apple
3 oz. piña colada mix

Blend and serve.

APPLE PUCKERITA

3/4 oz. Jose Cuervo tequila
1/2 oz. DeKuyper Pucker sour apple
sweet & sour mix
dash lime juice

Shake with ice and serve in a tall glass.

APPLE RUM FIZZ

1 1/4 oz. DeKuyper Pucker sour apple
3/4 oz. Bacardi rum
1/2 oz. Rose's grenadine
2 oz. sweet & sour mix

Top with lemon-lime soda.

APPLE SOUR

1 1/4 oz. DeKuyper Pucker sour apple
3 1/4 oz. sweet & sour mix

Shake with ice and serve.

APPLE SPAZZ

3/4 oz. DeKuyper Pucker sour apple
1 oz. DeKuyper Razzmatazz
2 oz. sweet & sour mix

Top with lemon-lime soda.

APPLE STONE SOUR

1 1/4 oz. DeKuyper Pucker sour apple
3 1/4 oz. sweet & sour mix

Top with orange juice.

APPLE TAZZ

3/4 oz. DeKuyper Pucker sour apple
1/2 oz. DeKuyper Razzmatazz
3/4 oz. Vox vodka
2 oz. sweet & sour mix

Top with lemon-lime soda.

APPLE TAZZ TEA

1/2 oz. DeKuyper Pucker sour apple
1/2 oz. DeKuyper Razzmatazz
1/2 oz. Vox vodka
1/2 oz. Cointreau
2 oz. sweet & sour mix

Top with cranberry juice.

APPLE VANILLA POP

DeKuyper Thrilla Vanilla
DeKuyper Pucker sour apple

Blend.

APPLE-ADE

2 parts DeKuyper Pucker sour apple
1 part Vox vodka

Pour over ice in a tall glass. Fill with lemonade.

APPLE-BERRY PUCKER

Equal parts:
DeKuyper Cheri-Beri and DeKuyper Pucker sour apple;
or DeKuyper Pucker sour apple and cranberry juice.

APPLE-CRANBERRY SPRITZER

1 oz. DeKuyper Pucker sour apple
1/2 oz. Vox vodka
4 oz. lemon-lime soda
1 1/2 oz. cranberry juice

Serve in a tall glass with ice.

APPLETINI

1 part DeKuyper Pucker sour apple
1 part Vox vodka

Served chilled in a martini glass. Garnish with an apple slice.

APRICOT ALEXANDER

1 oz. DeKuyper apricot brandy
1 oz. DeKuyper white crème de cacao
4 oz. vanilla ice cream

Mix in a blender until smooth. Pour into a wine glass.

APRICOT SOUR

2 tbsp. lemon juice
1/2 tsp. superfine sugar
2 oz. DeKuyper apricot brandy
3–4 ice cubes

Combine all ingredients in a shaker and shake vigorously. Strain into a chilled cocktail glass. Garnish with an orange slice and a maraschino cherry.

APRICOT SOURBALL

1 1/2 oz. DeKuyper apricot brandy
juice 1/2 lemon
juice 1/2 orange

In an on-the-rocks glass with ice, top with lemon and orange juices.

AQUATINI

1 part DeKuyper Pucker Island Blue schnapps
1 part Vox vodka

Served chilled in a martini glass with a lemon twist.

ARMORED CAR

1 oz. Disaronno amaretto
1 oz. Jose Cuervo tequila

Pour over ice in a rocks glass. Garnish with a lime slice.

ASTI COSMO

Combine 1 oz. cranberry juice, 1/4 oz. Rose's lime juice, and a splash of Cointreau in a chilled shaker and strain into a martini glass. Top with Martini & Rossi Asti.

ASTI HONEYDEW

Combine 1 1/2 oz. DeKuyper melon liqueur and 3 oz. lemonade in a chilled shaker and strain into a highball glass. Top with Martini & Rossi Asti.

ASTI KIR

Pour 1 oz. DeKuyper crème de cassis into a 6 oz. flute and gently top with 5 oz. Martini & Rossi Asti.

ASTI SOUR

Combine 1 1/2 oz. Disaronno amaretto and 2 oz. sweet & sour mix in a chilled shaker and strain into a highball glass. Top with Martini & Rossi Asti and garnish with an orange slice or cherry.

ATOMIC GREEN

1/4 oz. DeKuyper crème de banana liqueur
1/2 oz. DeKuyper melon liqueur
1/2 oz. DeKuyper Peachtree schnapps
1/2 oz. Vox vodka
1 oz. cream

Shake with ice. Strain and serve straight up.

AUNT ROSE

1 1/4 oz. Irish Mist
2 oz. cranberry juice
2 oz. orange juice

Shake. Serve in a tall glass with ice.

AUNT TILLIE'S APPLE TEA

Brew a nice cup of tea and top liberally with Laird's applejack. Squeeze in a wedge of lemon.

AVALANCHE

1 1/2 oz. Carolans Irish cream liqueur, splash cold milk, 1 scoop vanilla ice cream. Blend.

AZUL LEMONADE

1 1/4 parts DeKuyper Pucker Island Blue schnapps
1 lemon squeezed
2 parts sweet & sour mix
1 sugar packet

Serve over ice and garnish with a lemon twist.

B&B COFFEE

1 1/4 oz. B&B liqueur
4 oz. hot coffee

Top with whipped cream.

B&B

1 oz. Benedictine
1 oz. brandy

Stir and serve in a snifter.

B-52 WITH BOMBAY DOORS

1 part DeKuyper coffee liqueur
1 part Carolans Irish cream
1 part Cointreau
1 part Bombay Sapphire gin

Shake with ice and strain into a shot glass.

B-52

1 oz. DeKuyper coffee liqueur
1 oz. Carolans Irish cream
1 oz. Cointreau

Layer coffee liqueur, Carolans, and Cointreau into a large shot glass.

BABY BABY

2 oz. orange juice
1 oz. Vox vodka
1 oz. Cointreau

Pour orange juice, Vox vodka, and Cointreau into a tumbler glass with ice. Stir.

BACARDI & COLA

1 1/2 oz. Bacardi light or dark rum
3 oz. cola

Pour rum into tall glass filled with ice. Fill with your favorite cola and garnish with a squeeze of a lemon.

BACARDI & TONIC

1 1/4 oz. Bacardi light rum
tonic

Pour rum into a tall glass filled with ice. Fill with tonic.

BACARDI BLOSSOM

1 1/4 oz. Bacardi light rum
1 oz. orange juice
1/2 oz. lemon juice
1/2 tsp. sugar

Blend with crushed ice and pour. Garnish with a spring flower.

BACARDI BUCK

1 1/4 oz. Bacardi light or Añejo rum
ginger ale

Pour rum in a highball glass filled with ice. Add ginger ale and garnish with a twist of lemon peel.

BACARDI CHAMPAGNE COCKTAIL

1 oz. Bacardi Select rum
champagne
1 tsp. sugar
dash bitters

In a tall glass, mix rum, sugar, and bitters. Fill with champagne.

BACARDI COCKTAIL

1 1/4 oz. Bacardi light rum
1 oz. Rose's lime juice
1/2 tsp. sugar
1/2 oz. Rose's grenadine

Mix in a shaker with ice and strain into a chilled cocktail glass.

The New York Supreme Court ruled in 1936 that a Bacardi Cocktail is not a Bacardi Cocktail unless it's made with Bacardi rum.

BACARDI COLLINS

2 oz. Bacardi light rum
2 tsp. frozen lemonade or limeade concentrate
1/2 tsp. sugar
club soda

Combine first two ingredients in a tall glass with ice. Fill with club soda.

BACARDI DAIQUIRI

1 1/4 oz. Bacardi light rum
1/2 oz. lemon juice
1/2 tsp. sugar

Mix in shaker with ice and strain into a chilled cocktail glass.

BACARDI DRY MARTINI

2 oz. Bacardi light rum
1/2 oz. Martini & Rossi dry vermouth

Shake with ice and strain.

BACARDI FIRESIDE

1 1/4 oz. Bacardi light or dark rum
1 tsp. sugar
hot tea

In a mug, add sugar and rum. Fill with very hot tea and one cinnamon stick. Stir.

BACARDI FIZZ

1 1/4 oz. Bacardi light rum
1/4 oz. lemon juice
1/4 oz. Rose's grenadine
club soda

Pour rum and lemon juice in a highball glass filled with ice. Add the grenadine and fill with club soda.

BACARDI GINGER-N-SPICE

1 1/2 oz. Bacardi Spice rum
ginger ale

In a tall glass with ice, add rum and fill with ginger ale.

BACARDI HEMINGWAY

1 1/2 oz. Bacardi light rum
juice of 1/2 lime
1/4 oz. grapefruit juice
1/4 oz. maraschino liqueur

Mix with ice and serve. Ernest Hemingway would have written about this one.

BACARDI HOT BUTTERED RUM

In a mug put 1 tsp. sugar, 1/2 tsp. butter, 1 jigger Bacardi light or dark rum, 4 cloves. Fill with boiling water. Stir.

BACARDI HOT COFFEE

Add 1 1/2 oz. Bacardi light or dark rum to a cup of coffee. Whipped cream optional.

BACARDI LIMÓN COSMOPOLITAN

2 oz. Bacardi Limón
1 oz. Cointreau
1/2 oz. lime juice
cranberry juice

Garnish with a lemon twist.

BACARDI LIMÓN MARTINI

2 oz. Bacardi Limón
dash Martini & Rossi extra dry vermouth
splash cranberry juice

Stir in a cocktail glass. Garnish with a lemon. It's a new twist on an old classic. First invented at the Heart and Soul in San Francisco, CA.

BACARDI MARTINI COCKTAIL

1 1/2 oz. Bacardi rum
dash Martini & Rossi extra dry vermouth

Add olive.

BACARDI MOJITO

1 1/2 oz. Bacardi light rum
6 mint leaves
1/2 lime
2 dashes Angostura bitters
club soda

In a collins glass, place mint leaves and lime. Crush well with the back of a spoon. Add bitters and sugar. Fill glass with ice. Add rum and top with club soda. Stir well and garnish with a sprig of mint or lime wheel.

BACARDI O COFFEE

2 oz. Bacardi O
3 oz. hot coffee

Serve in a cup. Top with Carolans Irish cream.

BACARDI O COFFEE II

2 oz. Bacardi O
3 oz. hot coffee
splash Carolans Irish cream
splash DeKuyper green crème de menthe

Serve in a cup. Top with Carolans Irish cream and green crème de menthe.

BACARDI O TINI

1 1/2 oz. Bacardi O
3/4 oz. pineapple juice

Shake and serve in a chilled glass. Float Chambord.

BACARDI PINK SQUEEZE

1 1/2 oz. Bacardi light rum
pink lemonade

Pour rum into tall glass filled with ice. Fill with pink lemonade.

BACARDI RUM CAPPUCCINO

1 1/2 oz. Bacardi dark rum
coffee
1 tsp. sugar
ground cinnamon
whipped cream

Combine the rum and sugar in a glass. Add equal parts hot coffee and milk. Top with steamed milk, whipped cream, and cinnamon.

BACARDI SPICE CARIBBEAN MARTINI

2 1/2 oz. Bacardi spice rum
1/2 oz. DeKuyper crème de banana liqueur

Shake and strain. Serve straight up. Garnish with a pineapple wedge.

BACARDI SUNSET

1 1/4 oz. Bacardi light rum
3 oz. orange juice
squeeze lime

Combine in a tall glass with crushed ice. Add a squeeze of lime. Garnish with an orange wheel.

BACARDI SWEET MARTINI

2 oz. Bacardi light rum
1/2 oz. Martini & Rossi Rosso vermouth

Stir gently with ice in a cocktail glass.

BACARDI TU TU CHERRY

1 oz. Bacardi rum
1/4 oz. DeKuyper cherry liqueur
2 oz. orange juice
3 oz. cranberry juice

Shake with ice.

BACARDI YEAH MARTINI
COCKTAIL

1 1/2 oz. Bacardi O
2 1/2oz. pineapple juice
1 1/2 oz. cranberry juice
splash soda

*Serve straight up in a chilled glass; garnish with a lime
and maraschino cherry.*

BACK IN BLACK

1 oz. Cointreau
1 1/2 oz. Jose Cuervo tequila
cola

Pour Cointreau and Cuervo into a tumbler glass with ice.
Fill with cola. Stir.

BACKDRAFT

1 oz. Drambuie
1 oz. Cointreau

Serve as a shot.

BAGPIPE

1 1/4 oz. Dewar's scotch
hot coffee

Top with whipped cream or ice cream.

BALALAÏKA

1/2 oz. lemon juice
1/2 oz. Cointreau
1 1/2 oz. Vox vodka

Shake lemon juice, Cointreau, and Vox vodka with ice.
Strain into a cocktail glass.

BAMBOO COCKTAIL

1 1/2 oz. Sherry
3/4 oz. Martini & Rossi dry vermouth
dash Angostura bitters

Stir with ice and strain.

BANANA BOAT

3/4 oz. Bacardi rum
3/4 oz. DeKuyper crème de banana liqueur
1/4 oz. pineapple juice

Serve in a tall glass.

BANANA DAIQUIRI

1 1/4 oz. Bacardi light rum
1/4 oz. lemon juice or Rose's lime juice
1/2 tsp. sugar
1 banana, peeled

Blend.

BANANA MAN

1 oz. Bacardi light rum
1/4 oz. DeKuyper crème de banana liqueur
1/2 oz. lemon juice or
Rose's lime juice

Blend with ice and serve.

BANANA MARTINI

2 1/2 oz. Vox vodka
splash DeKuyper crème de banana liqueur
splash Martini & Rossi extra dry vermouth

Serve over ice with a banana slice.

BANANA RUM CREAM

1 1/2 oz. Bacardi dark rum
1/2 oz. DeKuyper crème de banana liqueur
1 oz. light cream

Shake well. Serve straight up or with ice.

BANANA SPLIT

DeKuyper Pucker Cheri-Beri and DeKuyper crème de banana mixed. Serve in a lowball glass with ice, garnished with whipped cream, topped with a maraschino cherry.

BANILLA BOAT

1 oz. Drambuie
1/2 oz. DeKuyper crème de banana liqueur
4 oz. vanilla ice cream
splash Chambord

Blend until smooth. Serve in a champagne glass. Pour Chambord over top. Garnish with a banana slice.

BANSHEE

3/4 oz. DeKuyper crème de banana liqueur
3/4 oz. DeKuyper light crème de cacao
3 oz. cream

Blend with crushed ice. Serve in a tulip glass.

BARBERRY COAST

1 1/4 oz. Chambord
1 1/2 oz. cranberry juice
1/2 oz. grapefruit juice

Serve over ice in a tall glass.

BARN BURNER

1 1/2 oz. Southern Comfort
small cinnamon stick
slice lemon peel
hot cider

Put cinnamon, lemon peel, and Southern Comfort in mug; fill with hot cider; stir.

BARRACUDA

1 1/4 oz. Bacardi dark rum
1 oz. pineapple juice
1/2 oz. Rose's lime juice
1/4 tsp. sugar
champagne

Shake everything but the champagne. Serve in a champagne glass and fill to the top with champagne.

BASIN STREET

2 oz. Knob Creek bourbon
1/2 oz. Cointreau
1 oz. lemon juice

Shake well with cracked ice and strain into a cocktail glass.

BAY BREEZE

2 parts Vox vodka
4 parts cranberry juice
2 parts pineapple juice

Shake ingredients with ice and strain into an ice-filled glass.

BEACH BUM

1 oz. Vox vodka
1 1/2 oz. DeKuyper melon liqueur
1 oz. cranberry juice

Mix in a shaker with ice. Strain.

BEACH COMBER

1 1/2 oz. Bacardi light rum
3/4 oz. Rose's lime juice
1/4 oz. Cointreau
dash maraschino liqueur

Shake. Serve straight up or with ice.

BEACH PARTY

1 1/4 oz. Bacardi light or dark rum
1 oz. pineapple juice
1 oz. orange juice
1 oz. Rose's grenadine

Blend with ice.

BEACHED WHALE

1/2 oz. Cointreau
1/2 oz. DeKuyper white crème de cacao
1 oz. advocaat

Shake with ice; serve in a rocks glass.

BEAM ME UP SCOTTY

Equal parts: Carolans Irish cream, DeKuyper coffee liqueur, DeKuyper crème de banane.

BEE'S KISS

1 oz. Bacardi light rum
1/4 oz. Bacardi dark rum
3/4 oz. cream
2 tsp. honey

Shake. Serve over ice.

BELGIAN COFFEE

Cointreau, Carolans Irish cream, hot coffee

BELLINI EASY

1 oz. DeKuyper Peachtree schnapps
3 oz. champagne

Pour schnapps in a champagne glass and add champagne.

BELLINI TINI

Bacardi O, peach nectar, splash of orange juice,
splash of champagne. Serve in a glass with the
rim dipped in strawberry juice.

Butterfield 8
Chicago, IL

BELLISIMO MARTINI

1 oz. Disaronno amaretto
1 oz. Bacardi O
splash cranberry juice

Stir with ice and strain into a martini glass.

BERI-BERI

Equal parts: DeKuyper Pucker Cheri-Beri, Vox vodka.

Serve on the rocks.

BERMUDA ROSE

1 oz. Bombay Sapphire gin
1/4 oz. DeKuyper apricot brandy
1/2 oz. Rose's lime juice
dash Rose's grenadine

Shake with ice and strain.

BETWEEN THE SHEETS

1 part Cointreau
1 part Hennessy cognac
1 part Bacardi light rum
dash lemon juice

Shake with ice. Strain into a sugar-rimmed glass.

BIG SLOPPY WET KISS

1 part DeKuyper Pucker Cheri-Beri
1 part DeKuyper Pucker sour apple
1 part DeKuyper Pucker grape schnapps
splash sweet & sour mix

Top with lemon-lime soda.

BIKINI MARTINI

2 oz. Bombay Sapphire gin
1/4 oz. freshly squeezed lime juice
1/4 oz. DeKuyper blue curacao
1/4 oz. DeKuyper Peachtree schnapps
sugar syrup

Shake and strain into a martini glass.

BITCH ON WHEELS

1/4 oz. Martini & Rossi extra dry vermouth
1 oz. Bombay Sapphire gin
1/4 oz. Pernod
1/4 oz. DeKuyper white crème de menthe

*Shake ingredients with ice and strain into a chilled cock-
tail glass.*

*Invented at Stars
San Francisco, CA*

BLACK BOMBAY SAPPHIRE GIN

1 1/2 oz. Bombay Sapphire gin
1/2 oz. black sambuca
2 tsp. Martini & Rossi Rosso vermouth

Shake. Strain into a cocktail glass and serve.

BLACK BUCK

1 1/4 oz. Bacardi dark rum
ginger ale

Pour rum in a tall glass with ice. Fill with ginger ale and garnish with a lemon.

BLACK DEVIL

1 1/2 oz. Bacardi light rum
1/2 oz. Martini & Rossi dry vermouth
1 pitted black olive

Stir well with ice and strain into a martini glass.

BLACK ICE

1 oz. black sambuca
1 oz. Vox vodka
1/4 oz. DeKuyper crème de menthe

Shake with ice and strain. You can also serve this one over ice in a highball glass.

BLACK MAGIC

1 1/2 oz. Vox vodka
3/4 oz. DeKuyper coffee liqueur
dash lemon juice

Shake with cracked ice. Add a dash of lemon juice.

BLACK ORCHID

1 oz. Vox vodka
1/2 oz. DeKuyper blue curacao
1 1/2 oz. cranberry juice

Build over ice in a 7 oz. rocks glass.

BLACK RUSSIAN

1 1/2 oz. Vox vodka
3/4 oz. DeKuyper coffee liqueur

Add Vox vodka and then DeKuyper coffee liqueur to a glass filled with cubed ice. Stir briskly. Garnish with a swizzle stick. Add cream for a White Russian.

BLACK SUN

1/2 oz. Bacardi light rum
cola
1 1/2 oz. Cointreau

*Pour Bacardi and Cointreau into tumbler glass with ice.
Fill with cola. Stir.*

BLACK TARTAN

1/4 oz. Drambuie
1 oz. Dewar's scotch
1/4 oz. Tullamore Dew Irish whiskey
1/4 oz. DeKuyper coffee liqueur

Shake. Serve over rocks.

BLACK TRUFFLE MARTINI

2 oz. Bombay Sapphire gin
splash Martini & Rossi extra dry vermouth
1 fresh, clean black truffle

*Mix ingredients with cracked ice in shaker; strain into a
martini glass. Garnish with a small, fresh black truffle.*

BLACK VELVET (A.K.A. BISMARCK OR CHAMPAGNE VELVET)

1 part Guinness stout
1 part champagne

Layer the champagne over the Guinness in a champagne flute.

BLACKTHORN

1 1/2 oz. Tullamore Dew Irish whiskey
1 1/2 oz. Martini & Rossi dry vermouth
3-4 dashes Pernod
3-4 dashes Angostura bitters

Shake or blend with ice. Pour into a chilled rocks glass.

BLARNEY COCKTAIL

1 1/2 oz. Tullamore Dew Irish whiskey
1 oz. Martini & Rossi dry vermouth
splash DeKuyper green crème de menthe

Shake well with ice. Strain into a cocktail glass. Serve with a green cherry.

BLARNEY STONE COCKTAIL

2 oz. Tullamore Dew Irish whiskey
1/2 tsp. Pernod
1/2 tsp. Cointreau
1/4 tsp. Rose's grenadine
dash Angostura bitters

Shake with ice and strain. Serve with a twist of orange peel and add an olive.

BLIGHTER BOB

1 oz. Bacardi light rum
1/2 oz. Bacardi dark rum
1/2 oz. DeKuyper crème de cassis
1 oz. orange juice
2 dashes orange bitters
2 oz. ginger ale

Stir and serve straight up or with ice. Garnish with a lemon twist.

BLIZZARD

1 1/4 oz. Vox vodka
Fresca

Serve in a tall glass with ice. Garnish with a twist of lemon.

BLONDE MARTINI

Bombay Sapphire. Enliven with Lillet Blonde.

Brasserie Jo Martini's
Chicago, IL

BLOODY BULL

1 1/4 oz. Vox vodka
2 1/2 oz. tomato juice
1 1/2 oz. beef bouillon
1–2 tsp. lemon juice
dash Worcestershire sauce
dash Tabasco sauce
dash pepper

Combine with ice in a shaker. Strain into a coffee glass.

BLOODY CAESAR

1 1/4 oz. Vox vodka
2 1/2oz. clamato juice
dash Worcestershire sauce
dash Tabasco sauce
dash salt and pepper

Pour Vox vodka into a glass with ice and fill with clamato juice. Add a dash of Tabasco, Worcestershire, pepper, and salt. Garnish with a celery stalk or a lime wheel.

BLUE DIABLO

1 part Jose Cuervo Clásico
4 parts lemon-lime soda
splash DeKuyper blue curacao

*Combine Cuervo and lemon-lime soda in a rocks glass
with ice. Add splash of blue curacao. Garnish with sugar
on the rim.*

BLUE HOOTER

1 part DeKuyper Pucker Island Blue schnapps
1 part DeKuyper Pucker watermelon schnapps

Serve as a shot.

BLUE LADY

1 oz. Bombay Sapphire gin
1/4 oz. DeKuyper blue curacao
1 oz. lemon mix

Shake. Serve over ice.

BLUE LAGOON

1 1/2 oz. Vox vodka
1/2 oz. DeKuyper blue curacao
3 oz. lemonade

Combine ingredients over ice in a highball glass.

BLUE LAGOON MARTINI

1 1/4 oz. Bacardi Limón
1/2 oz. DeKuyper blue curacao
1/4 oz. Martini & Rossi dry vermouth

Garnish with a strawberry or olives.

Alex Refojo
Club Mystique
Miami, FL

BLUE MONDAY

1/2 oz. Bombay Sapphire gin
1 1/2 oz. Cointreau
soda water

Pour Bombay Sapphire gin and Cointreau into a tumbler glass with ice. Fill with soda water. Add a drop of blue curacao. Stir.

BLUE RIBAND

1 1/2 oz. Bombay Sapphire gin
1/4 oz. Cointreau
1/4 oz. DeKuyper blue curacao

BLUE SHARK MARTINI

1 1/2 oz. Vox vodka
1 1/2 oz. Jose Cuervo tequila
1/2 oz. DeKuyper blue curacao

Shake and strain into a martini glass or over ice.

BLUE VELVET

1 part DeKuyper Pucker Island Blue schnapps
1 part Vox vodka
1 part Cointreau
splash lime
splash cranberry juice

Garnish with a lime wedge.

BLUEBERRY TEA

Cointreau, Disaronno amaretto, and hot tea.

Garnished with an orange slice.

BLUEBERRY SAPPHIRE

1 oz. Bombay Sapphire gin
1 oz. DeKuyper blueberry schnapps

Mix ingredients with cracked ice in shaker; strain into martini glass. Top with sweet & sour mix, DeKuyper blue curacao (for color), and blueberries.

Served at Lola Bar
Los Angeles, CA

BOBBY BURNS

1 1/2 oz. Dewar's White Label
1/2 oz. Martini & Rossi Rosso vermouth
3 dashes Benedictine

A version of the classic Rob Roy. Build in a cocktail glass over ice. Stir and serve.

BOCCI BALL

1/2 oz. Disaronno amaretto
1/2 oz. Vox vodka
1/2 oz. orange juice

Shake with ice. Serve straight up in a shot glass. You can also serve this one over ice in a rocks glass.

BOILERMAKER

1 1/4 oz. Tullamore Dew Irish whiskey
10 oz. beer

Serve whiskey in a shot glass with a glass of beer.

BOMBAY CLOUD

2 oz. Bombay Sapphire gin
1/4 oz. DeKuyper apricot brandy
1 oz. orange juice
grenadine syrup

BOMBAY SAPPHIRE GIN ALEXANDER

1 part Bombay Sapphire gin
1 part DeKuyper white crème de cacao
3 parts half-and-half

Shake with ice and serve straight up or on the rocks. Dust with nutmeg.

BOMBAY SAPPHIRE GIN AND CRAN

1 1/4 oz. Bombay Sapphire gin
2 1/2 oz. cranberry juice

Serve on the rocks.

BOMBAY SAPPHIRE GIN AND PINK

2 oz. Bombay Sapphire gin
3 oz. tonic water
dash bitters
lemon peel

Pour into a tall glass with ice. Add a lemon peel garnish.

BOMBAY SAPPHIRE GIN AND SIN

1 1/4 oz. Bombay Sapphire gin
1/4 oz. orange juice
1/4 oz. lemon juice
2 dashes grenadine

Shake Bombay, orange juice, lemon juice, and grenadine with ice. Strain into a chilled cocktail glass.

BOMBAY SAPPHIRE GIN AND TONIC

2 oz. Bombay Sapphire gin
3 oz. tonic

In a tall glass filled with ice, add Bombay and fill with tonic. Add a squeeze of lime.

BOMBAY SAPPHIRE GIN APPLE TONIC

1 part Bombay Sapphire gin
1 1/2 parts DeKuyper Pucker sour apple

Pour over ice in a tall glass. Fill with tonic.

BOMBAY SAPPHIRE GIN CASSIS

3 parts Bombay Sapphire gin
1 part DeKuyper crème de cassis

Stir on the rocks.

BOMBAY SAPPHIRE GIN COCKTAIL (AKA DUBONNET COCKTAIL)

1 part Bombay Sapphire gin
2 parts Dubonnet

Stir on the rocks. Add a lemon twist.

BOMBAY SAPPHIRE GIN DRIVER

1 1/4 oz. Bombay Sapphire gin
4 oz. orange juice
tonic water

Serve in a tall glass filled with ice.

BOMBAY SAPPHIRE GIN FIZZ

2 oz. Bombay Sapphire gin
1 tsp. sugar
juice of 1 lemon
club soda

Shake first three ingredients with ice and strain. Fill with club soda.

BOMBAY SAPPHIRE GINGER COLADA

1 1/2 oz. Coco Lopez cream of coconut
1 oz. Canton Delicate ginger liqueur
1/2 oz. Bombay Sapphire gin
1/2 oz. Bacardi rum

Blend.

BOMBAY SAPPHIRE GIN JULEP

1 1/4 oz. Bombay Sapphire gin
4 sprigs of mint
1 tsp. sugar

In a highball glass filled with shaved ice, stir until glass is frosted. Garnish with fresh mint.

BOMBAY SAPPHIRE GINOLANS

2 parts Carolans Irish cream
1 part Bombay Sapphire gin

Stir.

BOMBAY SAPPHIRE GIN OLD FASH-IONED

1 1/4 oz. Bombay Sapphire gin
2 dashes bitters
1/4 tsp. sugar
club soda

Crush (muddle) orange slice, bitters, and cherry on the bottom of a rocks glass. Add ingredients; fill with ice and club soda.

BOMBAY SAPPHIRE GIN RICKEY

1 1/4 oz. Bombay Sapphire gin
club soda

In a tall glass filled with ice, add Bombay and fill with club soda. Add a squeeze of lime.

BOMBAY SAPPHIRE GIN
SCREWDRIVER

1 1/4 oz. Bombay Sapphire gin
orange juice

In a tall glass filled with ice, add Bombay and fill with orange juice.

BOMBAY SAPPHIRE MARTINI

1 1/2 oz. Bombay Sapphire gin
dash Martini & Rossi extra dry vermouth

Shake with ice. Strain and serve straight up or on the rocks with some ice in a cocktail glass. Add a lemon twist or olive.

BONBINI

1 oz. Bacardi light or dark rum
1/4 oz. DeKuyper orange curacao
dash bitters

Stir and serve with ice.

BOOTLEGGER MARTINI

2 oz. Bombay Sapphire gin
1/4 oz. Southern Comfort

Stir gently with ice; serve straight up or over ice. Garnish with a lemon twist.

Chianti Restaurant
Houston, TX

BOSTON BREEZE

1 oz. Coco Lopez cream of coconut
1 1/4 oz. Bacardi rum
3 oz. cranberry juice
1 cup ice

Blend and serve in a margarita glass.

BOURBON AND WATER

2 oz. Knob Creek bourbon
2 1/2 oz. water

Pour bourbon and water into an old-fashioned glass. Add ice and a twist of lemon peel, if desired, and stir.

BOURBON HIGHBALL

2 oz. Knob Creek bourbon
3 oz. ginger ale or club soda

Fill a highball glass with bourbon, ginger ale or club soda, and ice cubes. Add a twist of lemon peel, if desired, and stir.

BOURBON ON THE ROCKS

2 oz. Knob Creek bourbon

Pour over ice slowly.

BOW STREET SPECIAL

1 1/2 oz. Tullamore Dew Irish whiskey
3/4 oz. Cointreau
1 oz. lemon juice

Shake or blend and strain into a chilled cocktail glass.

BRAIN HEMORRHAGE

3 parts Carolans Irish cream
1 part DeKuyper Peachtree schnapps
dash Rose's grenadine

Combine in a shot glass.

BRAINSTORM

1 3/4 oz. Tullamore Dew Irish whiskey
1/4 oz. Martini & Rossi dry vermouth
dash Benedictine

*Stir all ingredients and strain into a cocktail glass.
Decorate with a twist of orange peel.*

BRANDY ALEXANDER

1 1/2 oz. brandy or Hennessy cognac
1/2 oz. DeKuyper dark crème de cacao
1 oz. sweet cream or ice cream

Shake or blend with ice. Strain.

BRANDY EGGNOG

2–3 oz. Hennessy cognac
1/2 oz. superfine sugar or to taste
1 cup milk
1 beaten egg
freshly ground nutmeg

*Shake with ice or blend and strain into a chilled martini
glass or cup. Sprinkle with nutmeg.*

BRANDY FIX

2–3 oz. Hennessy cognac
1 tsp. sugar
1 tsp. water
juice of 1/2 lemon

Pour into an old-fashioned glass and fill with ice. Stir.

BRANDY FIZZ

2–3 oz. Hennessy cognac
1 1/2 oz. lemon juice or half lime and lemon juice
1/2 oz. sugar syrup (or to taste)
club soda

Shake and pour into a highball glass, fill with club soda.

BRASS KNUCKLE

1 oz. Knob Creek bourbon
1/2 oz. Cointreau
2 oz. sweetened lemon

Mix. Shake with ice and serve in a highball glass with ice.

BRAVE BULL

1 1/2 oz. Jose Cuervo tequila
1/2 oz. DeKuyper coffee liqueur

Stir and serve over ice.

BRAVO

1 oz. Vox vodka
1/2 oz. Campari

Pour Vox vodka and Campari over ice in a tall glass. Top with tonic. Garnish with a slice of lemon and lime.

BREAKFAST MARTINI

2 oz. Bombay Sapphire gin
1/8 oz. Martini and Rossi extra dry vermouth
1/2 oz. freshly squeezed lemon juice
1/8 tsp. orange marmalade
orange peel garnish

BRONX COCKTAIL

1/2 oz. Bombay Sapphire gin
2 tsp. Martini & Rossi extra dry vermouth
2 tsp. Martini & Rossi Rosso vermouth
2 oz. orange juice

Shake with ice. Serve over rocks.

BUBBLE GUM

1/2 oz. DeKuyper melon liqueur
1/2 oz. Vox vodka
1/2 oz. DeKuyper crème de banana
1/2 oz. orange juice
dash Rose's grenadine

Serve in a shot glass.

BUCK-A-ROO

1 1/4 oz. Bacardi light or dark rum
root beer

Pour rum into a collins glass filled with ice. Fill with root beer.

BUCKING IRISH

1 1/4 oz. Tullamore Dew Irish whiskey
5 oz. ginger ale

Combine in an ice-filled collins glass. Garnish with a lemon twist.

BULL AND BEAR

1 3/4 oz. Knob Creek bourbon
3/4 oz. Cointreau
1 tbs. Rose's grenadine
juice of 1/2 lime

Shake with cracked ice. Garnish with a maraschino cherry and an orange slice.

BULLSHOT

1 1/2 oz. Vox vodka
1 tsp. lemon juice
dash Worcestershire sauce
dash Tabasco sauce
4 oz. chilled beef bouillon
dash salt and pepper

Shake and serve in a glass. Garnish with a lemon wedge.

BUNGEE JUMPER

1 1/4 oz. Irish Mist
4 oz. orange juice
1/2 oz. cream
splash Disaronno amaretto

Mix all but the amaretto in a highball glass. Float the Disaronno amaretto on top.

BURNT RAYBIRD

1/2 oz. Disaronno amaretto
1/2 oz. DeKuyper dark crème de cacao
1/2 oz. DeKuyper coffee liqueur
hot coffee

Pour into a coffee mug.

BUSHRANGER

1 oz. Dubonnet
1 oz. Bacardi light rum
2 dashes Angostura bitters

Stir and serve over ice.

BUSHWHACKER

2 oz. Coco Lopez cream of coconut
2 oz. half-and-half
1 oz. DeKuyper coffee liqueur
1/2 oz. DeKuyper dark crème de cacao
1/2 oz. Bacardi rum
1 cup ice

Blend and serve in a margarita glass.

BUTTERSCOTCH COLLINS

1/2 oz. Drambuie
1 tsp. sugar
water
1 1/2 oz. Dewar's scotch
2 oz. lemon juice
1 oz. soda

Dissolve sugar in water. Pour over ice in collins glass. Add Dewar's, Drambuie, and lemon juice. Stir. Top with soda. Garnish with a maraschino cherry and an orange slice.

BUTTERY NIPPLE

1/3 oz. Carolans Irish cream
1/3 oz. Vox vodka
1/3 oz. DeKuyper butterscotch schnapps

Combine in a shot glass.

CAFE AMARETTO

1 oz. Disaronno amaretto
1/2 oz. DeKuyper coffee liqueur
coffee

Pour into a mug or coffee cup.

CAFE CACAO

2 oz. DeKuyper crème de cacao
coffee

Top with whipped cream.

CAFE CARIBBEAN

1 oz. Disaronno amaretto
1 oz. Bacardi rum
3 oz. coffee
sugar to taste

Pour into a coffee cup or mug.

CAFE DISARONNO

1 1/2 oz. Disaronno amaretto
3 oz. coffee

Pour Disaronno amaretto into a coffee cup. Fill with hot coffee. Garnish with whipped cream and a sprinkling of cinnamon.

CAFE ITALIA

1 1/2 oz. Disaronno amaretto
Hennessy cognac

Fill with coffee. Top with whipped cream.

CAFÉ MEXICANO

1 oz. DeKuyper coffee liqueur
1/2 oz. Jose Cuervo tequila
hot coffee

Top with whipped cream.

CAIPIRINHA DE FRANCIA

1/2 glass limes, muddled
3/4 oz. sugar syrup
2 oz. Bacardi light rum

Serve in a tall glass.

CALIFORNIA COOLAID

1 1/4 oz. Bacardi light or Añejo rum
orange juice
milk

Pour Bacardi into a tall glass half-filled with ice. Add half orange juice and half milk. Stir.

CAMERON'S KICK

3/4 oz. Tullamore Dew Irish whiskey
3/4 oz. Dewar's scotch whisky
juice of 1/4 lemon
2 dashes Angostura bitters

Shake well with cracked ice and strain into a cocktail glass.

CAMPARI ORANGE

1/3 Campari
2/3 orange juice
ice cubes

Put ice in a glass. Add orange juice and Campari. Stir and serve.

CAMPARTINI

2 oz. Campari
2 oz. Vox vodka
dash Rose's lime juice
splash orange juice

Shake and serve with an orange slice in a tall glass.

CANADIAN COFFEE

1/2 oz. Canadian Club
1/2 oz. DeKuyper coffee liqueur
1/2 oz. Disaronno amaretto
hot coffee

Top with whipped cream and a maraschino cherry.

CANDY ASS

1 oz. Chambord
1 oz. DeKuyper chocolate liqueur

Shake with ice and strain into a shot glass.

CANTON SUNRISE

1 1/2 oz. Canton Delicate ginger liqueur
1 1/2 oz. orange juice
splash Rose's grenadine

Combine over ice.

CAPE CODDER

1 1/4 oz. Vox vodka
3 oz. cranberry juice
dash lime juice

Combine in a chilled cocktail glass over ice.

CAPE FRANCE

1 oz. Cointreau
1 oz. Vox vodka
3 oz. cranberry juice
lime wedge

In a tall glass, combine ingredients over ice and stir. Garnish with a wedge of lime.

CAPPUCCINO DISARONNO

Pour 1 1/2 oz. Disaronno amaretto into a coffee cup. Fill with fresh cappuccino.

CAPPUCCINO WITH BOMBAY SAPPHIRE GIN

Float 1/2 oz. Bombay Sapphire gin on top the foamy milk of a cup of cappuccino.

CARAMEL APPLE

2 parts DeKuyper Pucker sour apple
1 part DeKuyper ButterShots

Chill and serve as a shot.

CAROLANS DUBLIN DOUBLE

1 part Carolans Irish cream
1 part Disaronno amaretto

Serve in a shot glass.

CAROLANS FIZZ

1 part Carolans Irish cream
1 part soda water
fresh whipped cream
1/3 glass crushed ice

Pour over crushed ice. Add fresh whipped cream and serve.

CAROLANS CONCERTO COFFEE

Equal parts:
    Carolans Irish cream
    Tia Maria

Stir in coffee.

CAROLARETTO

1 part Carolans Irish cream
1 part Disaronno amaretto

Shake or stir on the rocks.

CASCADE MARTINI

1 1/2 parts Vox raspberry vodka
1 1/2 parts cranberry juice
1/2 part freshly squeezed lemon juice
1/4 part Chambord
1/4 part vanilla syrup
12 fresh raspberries

Shake all ingredients with ice and strain into a glass.

CASSIS COCKTAIL

1 oz. Knob Creek bourbon
1/2 oz. Martini & Rossi dry vermouth
1 tsp. DeKuyper crème de cassis

Shake with cracked ice. Strain into a chilled cocktail glass.

CAVALIER

1 1/2 oz. Jose Cuervo tequila
1/2 oz. Galliano
1 1/2 oz. orange juice
1/2 oz. cream

Shake with ice and strain into a cocktail glass.

CAZUELA

3 parts Jose Cuervo Especial
1 tsp. grenadine
lemon-lime soda
dash salt
1 slice lime and lemon
1 slice orange
1 slice grapefruit

Put salt, lime, orange, grapefruit, lemon, and ice in a cazuela (a clay bowl commonly found in La Barca, Jalisco, Mexico). NOTE: It is important to use a cazuela that is approximately 500 ml (15 oz.). Add grenadine and Jose Cuervo Especial. Then fill with lemon-lime soda and stir.

CELTIC BULL

1 1/2 oz. Tullamore Dew Irish whiskey
2 oz. beef consommé or bouillon
2 oz. tomato juice
1–2 dashes Worcestershire sauce
dash Tabasco sauce
dash freshly ground pepper

Shake and pour into a chilled highball glass.

This is a variation of the Bloody Bull, which is derived from the Bloody Mary.

CEMENT MIXER

3/4 shot Carolans Irish cream
1/4 shot lime juice

Pour ingredients directly into a glass. Let the drink stand for eight seconds.

CHAMBORD & CHAMPAGNE

1 oz. of Chambord at the bottom of a glass. Fill with champagne.

CHAMBORD & COFFEE

Add Chambord to a cup of coffee. Top with whipped cream.

CHAMBORD & COGNAC

1/2 Chambord
1/2 Hennessy cognac

Serve in a brandy snifter.

CHAMBORD & VOX VODKA SPLASH

1/2 oz. Vox vodka
1/2 oz. Chambord

Fill a martini glass half way with ice. Add sparkling water and garnish with an orange slice.

CHAMBORD ADRENALINE

1/2 oz. Chambord
1/2 oz. Vox vodka

Shake with ice. Strain into a shot glass.

CHAMBORD COLADA

1 1/2 oz. Chambord
1 1/2 oz. Bacardi rum
2 oz. pineapple juice
1/2 oz. Coco Lopez cream of coconut
3/4 cup ice

Blend.

CHAMBORD FROST

1 1/2 oz. Chambord
juice of 1/4 lemon
1 cup crushed ice

Blend or shake and pour into an ice-filled glass.

CHAMBORD ICEBERG

1/2 oz. Chambord
1/2 oz. Vox vodka

Combine in a champagne glass packed to the top with ice.

CHAMBORD KAMIKAZE

1 oz. Vox vodka
1/2 oz. Chambord
1/4 oz. Cointreau
1/4 oz. lime juice

Shake and strain into a shot glass.

CHAMBORD MARGARITA

1 1/2 oz. Jose Cuervo tequila
1/2 oz. Chambord
1 oz. Cointreau
juice of 1/2 lime

Blend with an equal amount of ice until smooth.

CHAMBORD MARTINI

1/2 oz. Chambord
2 1/2 oz. Vox vodka

Pour off the ice.

CHAMBORD MOJITO

1 oz. Chambord
1/2 glass limes, squeezed
5 mint leaves
3/4 oz. sugar syrup
2 oz. Bacardi light rum

Muddle mint leaves, fill with rum, Chambord, and ice in a tall glass. Top with club soda.

CHAMBORD PEACHY ROSE GIMLET

1 oz. Chambord
1 oz. Bombay gin
2 oz. sweet & sour mix
1 oz. peachy Rose mix (homemade puree peaches and
    essence of rose)
ice

Shake or stir and garnish with a lime.

CHAMBORD SIDECAR

1 1/2 oz. Hennessy cognac
1/2 oz. Cointreau
2 oz. sweet & sour mix
2 oz. Chambord

Shake with ice, strain into a sugar-rimmed martini glass.

CHAMBORD SPIRIT

1/2 oz. Chambord
1/2 oz. Wild Spirit

Pour over lots of ice.

CHAMBUIE

1/2 oz. Drambuie
3 oz. champagne

Pour Drambuie into a champagne flute. Top with champagne.

CHAMPAGNE COCKTAIL

3 oz. champagne, chilled
1 cube sugar
dash Angostura bitters

Stir ingredients slowly. Garnish with a lemon twist.

CHAMU

1/2 oz. Chambord
1 oz. Bacardi rum
1/2 oz. Vox vodka
3 oz. pineapple juice

Combine ingredients in a tall glass with ice. Fill with pineapple juice.

CHAPEL HILL

1 3/4 oz. Knob Creek bourbon
1/2 oz. Cointreau
1 tbsp. lemon juice

Shake with ice and strain into a cocktail glass. Add a twist of orange peel.

CHARRO NEGRO

2 parts Jose Cuervo Especial
cola
juice of 1/2 lemon
salt

Rub the rim of a chilled tall highball glass with lemon juice and dip it into the salt to coat. Put ice into the glass; add Jose Cuervo Especial and juice of half a lemon. Add some more salt if you'd like and fill the glass with cola.

CHERI APE

1 oz. DeKuyper Pucker Cheri-Beri
1/2 oz. DeKuyper blue curacao

Add ice; fill with sweet & sour mix.

CHERI

2 oz. DeKuyper Pucker Cheri-Beri
1/2 oz. Bacardi rum
lemon-lime soda

Serve in a glass, top with lemon-lime soda.

CHERI FIZZ

1 oz. DeKuyper Pucker Cheri-Beri
1/2 oz. DeKuyper San Tropique rum
splash lemon-lime soda

Add ice; fill with lemon-lime soda.

CHERI PUCKER JELLO SHOTS

2 oz. DeKuyper Pucker Cheri-Beri
ice
2 oz. orange juice

Pour Pucker on top. Let it filter through juice and stir.

CHERI ROYALE

DeKuyper Pucker Cheri-Beri
vanilla ice cream

Blend; serve in a lowball glass.

CHERI SODA

DeKuyper Pucker Cheri-Beri
DeKuyper Thrilla Vanilla
2 scoops vanilla ice cream

*Blend. Fill a soda glass with 3/4 oz. carbonated water.
Garnished with whipped cream. Top with a maraschino cherry.*

CHERI VANILLA POP

1 oz. DeKuyper Thrilla Vanilla
1 oz. DeKuyper Pucker Cheri-Beri

Serve as a shot or over ice.

CHERI-BERI COLADA

1 oz. DeKuyper Pucker Cheri-Beri
1 oz. Bacardi rum
fill piña colada mix

*Blend ingredients. Top with 1/2 oz. floater of DeKuyper
Pucker Cheri-Beri, garnish with a maraschino cherry.*

CHERI-BERI MARGARITA

*Normal margarita recipe but substitute DeKuyper Pucker
Cheri-Beri for Cointreau.*

CHERI-BOMB

1 oz. DeKuyper Pucker Cheri-Beri
1 oz. DeKuyper Hot Damn! schnapps

Serve as a shot.

CHERI-COLA

1 part DeKuyper Pucker Cheri-Beri

Fill glass with cola; serve as a mixed drink.

CHERRY BLOSSOM

2 oz. Hennessy cognac
3/4 oz. Cointreau
1/2 oz. DeKuyper cherry brandy
1/2 oz. lemon juice
1 oz. Rose's grenadine

Shake with ice and strain into a glass. Garnish with a maraschino cherry.

CHERRY BOMB

1/2 oz. DeKuyper cherry brandy
1 oz. Bacardi rum
1/2 oz. sweet & sour mix

Shake with ice and strain into a shot glass.

CHERRY CREAM

2 parts DeKuyper Pucker Cheri-Beri
1 part Bacardi spice rum

Fill with cream. Add a splash of club soda.

CHERRY ICE

1 1/2 oz. DeKuyper Pucker Cheri-Beri
4 oz. ice cream

Blend with ice.

CHERRY LIFESAVER

3/4 oz. Disaronno amaretto
3/4 oz. Vox vodka
1 oz. cranberry juice

Shake with ice; strain into a cocktail glass.

CHERRY POPPIN' PINATA

2 parts DeKuyper Pucker Cheri-Beri
2 parts Jose Cuervo tequila

Shake with ice; serve as a shot or over ice.

CHI CHI

1 1/2 oz. Vox vodka
3/4 oz. pineapple juice
1 1/2 oz. cream of coconut

Blend and add a maraschino cherry.

CHICAGO

2 oz. Hennessy cognac
1/4 oz. Cointreau
lemon wedge
superfine sugar
Angostura bitters
champagne

Shake with ice and strain into a wine glass. Fill with cold champagne.

CHICAGO MARTINI

2 1/2 oz. Vox vodka served in a glass rinsed with Cointreau.

CHICAGO STYLE

3/4 oz. Bacardi light rum
1/4 oz. Cointreau
1/4 oz. DeKuyper anisette
1/4 oz. lemon or lime juice

Blend with ice.

CHICAGO VIEW

2 oz. Bacardi O
1/2 oz. Chambord
2 oz. passion fruit juice

Shake with ice and serve over ice.

CHINA BEACH

3/4 oz. Canton Delicate ginger liqueur
1 oz. cranberry juice
splash Vox vodka

Shake with ice and serve over ice.

CHINESE TORTURE

1 part Canton Delicate ginger liqueur
1 part Bacardi 151 rum

Shake with ice and strain into a shot glass.

CHOCOLATE COVERED CHERI

3/4 oz. DeKuyper Pucker Cheri-Beri
1/2 oz. DeKuyper Thrilla Vanilla
1 1/2–2 oz. cream

Shake with ice; serve on the rocks.

CHOCOLATE MARTINI

1 oz. Vox vodka
1/2 oz. chocolate liqueur

Shake over ice; strain into a chilled cocktail glass.

CIDER AND TEQUILA HOT TODDY

1/2 cup Jose Cuervo Especial
4 cups apple cider
1 cup cranberry juice
1/4 cup Cointreau
lime slices

In a saucepan, heat cider and cranberry juice cocktail just until hot (do not let boil) and remove from heat. Stir in Jose Cuervo Especial and Cointreau. Serve toddies in mugs, garnished with lime slices. Makes about six cups.

CIDER SENSATION

1 oz. DeKuyper Pucker sour apple
3/4 oz. apple cider

Serve over ice.

CINNAMON APPLE MARGARITA

1 1/2 oz. Jose Cuervo tequila
1 oz. DeKuyper Pucker sour apple
3 oz. sweet & sour mix
1 oz. orange juice
2 oz. lemon-lime soda
1/2 oz. DeKuyper Hot Damn! schnapps

Blend all of the ingredients together, top with DeKuyper Hot Damn! schnapps.

CLAM VOYAGE

1 oz. Bacardi light or dark rum
1/4 oz. apple brandy
1 oz. orange juice
dash orange bitters

Blend with ice and serve in a margarita glass.

CLAMDIGGER

1 1/4 oz. Vox vodka
3 oz. Mott's clamato juice
dash Tabasco sauce
dash Worcestershire sauce

Combine in a mixing glass; stir well. Add ice and strain into a chilled old-fashioned glass. Garnish with a lemon peel.

CLARIDGE CLASSIC

2 oz. Bombay Sapphire gin
1/8 oz. Martini & Rossi extra dry vermouth
brine from cocktail olives
cocktail olives garnish

Shake with ice. Strain into a martini glass, add olive.

COCKTAIL NA MARA (COCKTAIL OF THE SEA)

2 oz. Tullamore Dew Irish whiskey
2 oz. clam juice
4 oz. tomato juice
1/2 oz. lemon juice
3–4 dashes Worcestershire sauce
dash Tabasco sauce
pinch white pepper

Stir all ingredients well in a mixing glass with cracked ice and pour into a chilled highball glass.

COCO COPA

Bacardi Coco, splashes of banana nectar, pineapple juice, white chocolate liqueur, and grenadine; served on ice with orange slice garnish, maraschino cherry, and flower pick.

CÓCO JUICE

3/4 oz. Bacardi rum
3/4 oz. Bombay Sapphire gin
1 oz. pineapple juice
1 oz. cranberry juice

Shake all ingredients with ice and pour over ice into a tall glass.

COCO LOCO (CRAZY COCONUT)

1 1/2 oz. Jose Cuervo tequila
3 oz. pineapple juice
2 oz. Coco Lopez cream of coconut

Blend. Garnish with a pineapple spear.

COCO MARGARITA

1 1/4 oz. Jose Cuervo 1800 tequila
1 oz. sweet & sour mix
1 1/2 oz. pineapple juice
1/2 oz. fresh lime juice
1/2 oz. Coco Lopez cream of coconut

Shake or blend ingredients. Garnish with fresh pineapple.

COCOLOU

1 part Carolans Irish cream
1 part DeKuyper crème de cacao

Stir well over ice.

COCOMISTICO

1/2 oz. Jose Cuervo Mistico tequila
1/2 oz. Carolans Irish cream
1/2 oz. chocolate liqueur
1 oz. half-and-half

Shake ingredients and strain into a rocks glass.

COCOMOTION

4 oz. Coco Lopez cream of coconut
2 oz. lime juice
1 1/2 oz. Bacardi dark rum

Blend and serve. Garnish with a maraschino cherry.

COCONUT BELLINI

2 oz. Coco Lopez cream of coconut
3 oz. champagne
2 oz. peach puree
1/2 oz. DeKuyper Peachtree schnapps
1 cup ice

Blend.

COCONUT PUNCH

1 1/4 oz. Bacardi light or Añejo rum
2 oz. Coco Lopez cream of coconut
1/2 oz. lemon juice
3–4 tbsp. vanilla ice cream

Mix all ingredients in a shaker or blender with crushed ice and pour into a tall glass.

COFFEE COCKTAIL

1 1/2 oz. Hennessy cognac
3/4 oz. Cointreau
1 oz. cold black coffee

Shake with ice and pour into a snifter.

COINTREAU GINI

1 1/2 oz. Cointreau
lemon-lime soda

Pour Cointreau into a tumbler glass with ice. Fill to the top with lemon-lime soda. Stir.

COINTREAU CAÏPIRINHA

1/2 lime
1 1/2 oz. Cointreau

Cut 1/2 of lime into five or six pieces. Crush the lime in the glass. Fill to the top with crushed ice. Fill with 1 1/2 oz. of Cointreau and stir.

COINTREAU CLIP

1/2 oz. lemon or lime juice
1 1/2 oz. Cointreau
grapefruit juice

Strain into a tumbler glass with ice. Fill with grapefruit juice. Stir. Shake lemon (or lime) juice and Cointreau with ice.

COINTREAU COLADA

1/2 oz. pineapple juice
1 oz. Cointreau
1 1/2 oz. Bacardi Cóco

Blend pineapple juice, Cointreau, and Bacardi Cóco with ice. Strain into a tumbler glass with ice. Stir. Add a drop of grenadine.

COINTREAU FIZZ

1 tsp. sugar (or sugarcane syrup)
juice of 1 lemon
1 1/2 oz. Cointreau
soda water

Shake sugar, fresh lemon juice, and Cointreau with ice. Strain into a tumbler glass. Fill with soda water.

COINTREAU GRAPEFRUIT

1 1/2 oz. Cointreau
grapefruit juice

Pour Cointreau in a tumbler glass with ice. Fill with grapefruit juice. Stir.

COINTREAU SANTA FE MARGARITA

1 1/2 oz. Jose Cuervo gold tequila
3/4 oz. Cointreau
2 oz. sweet & sour mix
2 oz. cranberry juice

Blend ingredients and serve in a margarita glass.

COINTREAU SPARKLE

1 oz. Cointreau
chilled sparkling white wine

Pour Cointreau into a champagne glass. Fill with chilled sparkling white wine.

COINTREAU STRAWBERRY MARGARITA

1 1/4 oz. Jose Cuervo gold tequila
3/4 oz. Cointreau
2 oz. sweet & sour mix
3 oz. frozen strawberries

Blend ingredients and serve in a margarita glass.

COINTREAU TONIC

1 1/2 oz. Cointreau
tonic water

Pour Cointreau into a tumbler glass full of ice. Fill with tonic water. Stir.

COINTREAU MARTINI

1/8 oz. Cointreau
2 oz. Vox vodka

Shake with ice. Serve over ice or straight up.

COLD IRISH

1 1/2 oz. Tullamore Dew Irish whiskey
1/2 oz. Irish Mist
2-3 drops DeKuyper crème de cacao
whipped cream
coffee soda

Pour the Tullamore Dew Irish whiskey and the Irish Mist over ice. Fill with coffee soda and stir. Touch up the whipped cream with the crème de cacao and use it to top the drink.

COLORADO BULLDOG

1 1/2 oz. DeKuyper coffee liqueur
4 oz. cream
splash cola

Pour first two ingredients over ice. Add a splash of cola. Stir.

COLUMBUS COCKTAIL

1 1/2 oz. Bacardi rum
3/4 oz. DeKuyper apricot brandy
juice of 1/2 lime

Mix or blend with crushed ice.

COMFORT & CREAM

1/2 oz. Southern Comfort
1/2 oz. Carolans Irish cream

Shake.

COMFORT COLADA

1 jigger (1 1/2 oz.) Southern Comfort
1 oz. Coco Lopez cream of coconut
2 oz. unsweetened pineapple juice

Shake with 1/2 cup crushed ice or use a blender.

COMFORT MOCHA

1 1/2 oz. Southern Comfort
1 tsp. instant cocoa or hot chocolate
1 tsp. instant coffee

Add boiling water. Top with whipped cream.

COMFORTING COFFEE

1 1/2 oz. Southern Comfort
1/2 oz. DeKuyper dark crème de cacao
coffee

COMMANDO FIX

2 oz. Tullamore Dew Irish whiskey
1/4 oz. Cointreau
1/2 oz. lime juice

Fill a glass with ice. Add Irish whiskey, Cointreau, and lime juice. Stir slowly.

COMMODORE

1 part Knob Creek bourbon
1 part DeKuyper crème de cacao
1 part sweetened lemon juice
dash Rose's grenadine

Shake with ice and serve over ice.

CONCHITA

1 1/4 oz. Jose Cuervo tequila
1/2 oz. lemon juice
6 oz. grapefruit juice

*Combine first two ingredients in a chilled highball glass.
Fill with grapefruit juice and stir.*

CONTINENTAL

1 oz. Bacardi light rum
1/4 oz. DeKuyper green crème de menthe
3/4 oz. Rose's lime juice
1/4 tsp. sugar (optional)

Blend with ice.

COOL MIST

2 oz. Irish Mist
tonic water

*Combine in a tall glass with crushed ice. Add a shamrock
for a garnish.*

COOPERHEAD

1 1/4 oz. Vox vodka
ginger ale

In a tall glass filled with ice, add a squeeze of lime and garnish with a lime wedge.

COPPER ILLUSION MARTINI

1/4 oz. Cointreau
1/4 oz. Campari
2 1/2 oz. Bombay Sapphire gin

Serve in a martini mixing glass filled with ice. Add on orange twist for garnish.

Michael Vezzoni
The Four Seasons Olympic Hotel
Seattle, WA

CORK COMFORT

1 1/2 oz. Tullamore Dew Irish whiskey
3/4 oz. Martini & Rossi Rosso vermouth
3-4 dashes Angostura bitters
3-4 dashes Southern Comfort

Shake with ice. Pour into a chilled rocks glass.

CORKSCREW

3/4 oz. Bacardi light rum
1/4 oz. brandy
1/4 oz. port wine
1/2 oz. lemon or Rose's lime juice

Stir. Serve over ice.

CORNET MARTINI

1 1/2 oz. Bombay Sapphire gin
dash wine

*Stir in cocktail glass. Strain and serve straight up or on
the rocks. Add a lemon twist or olives.*

CORPSE REVIVER

1 1/2 oz. Laird's applejack
3/4 oz. Hennessy cognac
1/2 oz. Martini & Rossi Rosso vermouth

Shake and strain into a chilled cocktail glass.

COSMO KAZI

4 parts Vox vodka
1 part Cointreau
dash lime juice
splash cranberry juice

Combine ingredients and pour over ice.

COSMOPOLITAN MARTINI

1 part Cointreau
2 parts Vox vodka
juice of 1/2 lime
splash cranberry juice

Shake with ice and strain.

COSSACK CHARGE

1 1/2 oz. Vox vodka
1/2 oz. Hennessey cognac
1/2 oz. DeKuyper cherry brandy

Mix all ingredients with cracked ice in a shaker or blender and pour into a chilled cocktail glass.

COW PUNCHER

1 oz. Bacardi light or dark rum
1 oz. DeKuyper white crème de cacao
milk

Pour Bacardi and crème de cacao into a tall glass half filled with ice. Fill with milk.

COWBOY MARTINI

2 oz. Bombay Sapphire gin
sugar syrup
fresh mint leaves
orange bitters

Shake with ice and strain into a martini glass.

CRAN-APPLE

1 oz. DeKuyper Pucker sour apple
1/2 oz. Vox vodka
cranberry juice

Serve as a shot or a drink.

CRANBERRY LARGO

1 1/2 oz. DeKuyper Key Largo tropical schnapps
cranberry juice

Pour Key Largo over ice into a highball glass. Add cranberry juice to fill. Garnish with a lemon or lime.

CRANBERRY MARGARITA

1 1/2 parts Jose Cuervo Especial
3 parts Jose Cuervo margarita mix
dash cranberry juice
handful of frozen cranberries

Blend all ingredients in a blender with one scoop of crushed ice. Pour entire contents into a margarita glass. NOTE: The cranberries should fleck throughout the drink.

CRANJACK

1 1/2 oz. Laird's applejack
4 oz. club soda
splash cranberry juice

Pour Laird's applejack over ice in a tall glass. Add club soda with a splash of cranberry juice. Garnish with lime if desired.

CRAN-RUM TWISTER

2 oz. Bacardi light rum
3 oz. cranberry juice
lemon-lime soda

Combine the first two ingredients in a tall glass with ice. Fill with lemon-lime soda and garnish with a lemon slice.

CRANTINI

2 oz. Bacardi Limón
touch Martini & Rossi extra dry vermouth
splash cranberry juice

Shake and serve straight up. Garnish with cranberries and a lemon twist.

CRAZY PUCKER

1 part DeKuyper Pucker sour apple
1 part DeKuyper Pucker Cheri-Beri
1 part DeKuyper Pucker grape schnapps
1 part Vox vodka
squeeze lime

Top with cola in a tall glass.

CREAM WHISKEY

1 part Carolans Irish cream
2 parts rye whiskey

Stir well over ice.

CREAMED IRISH COFFEE

2 oz. Carolans Irish cream
hot coffee

Add sugar to taste.

CREAMED SHERRY

2 parts Carolans Irish cream
1 part Duff Gordon cream
Sherry

Stir well over ice.

CREAMSICKLE

3/4 oz. Disaronno amaretto
3/4 oz. Cointreau
1/2 oz. orange juice
1 1/2 oz. cream

Blend with ice. Serve in a wine glass.

CREAMSICLE

1/2 oz. Cointreau
1/2 oz. Liquore Galliano
1 oz. cream
orange juice

Shake with ice and strain.

CREAMY IRISH COFFEE

1 1/2 oz. Carolans Irish cream

Fill with hot coffee. Top with whipped cream.

CREOLE

1 3/4 oz. Bacardi light rum
2 splashes lemon
3 1/2 oz. beef bouillon
dash pepper
dash salt
dash Tabasco sauce
dash Worcestershire sauce

Combine over ice.

CREOLE LADY

1 1/2 oz. Knob Creek bourbon
1 oz. madeira
1 tsp. grenadine

Stir with ice and strain into a cocktail glass. Serve with one green and one maraschino red cherry.

CREST OF THE WAVE

1 1/4 oz. Bombay Sapphire gin
1 1/2 oz. grapefruit juice
1 1/2 oz. cranberry juice

Shake with ice. Serve in a tall glass.

CRICKET

3/4 oz. Bacardi light rum
1/4 oz. DeKuyper white crème de cacao
1/4 oz. DeKuyper green crème de menthe
1 oz. cream

Blend.

CRISP SUNSET

2 oz. Bombay Sapphire gin
1 tbs. pineapple juice
1/2 oz. Cointreau

Mix ingredients with cracked ice in shaker; strain into a martini glass.

CUBA LIBRE

1 3/4 oz. Bacardi rum
cola
juice of 1/4 lime

Add Bacardi to a glass filled with ice. Fill with cola. Add lime juice and stir.

CUCARACHA

1/2 part Jose Cuervo Especial
1/2 part DeKuyper coffee liqueur

Pour Jose Cuervo Especial and DeKuyper coffee liqueur into a shot glass.

CUERVO AND TONIC

2 parts Jose Cuervo Especial
chilled tonic water
1/4 lime
2 thin lime slices
coarse salt

Rub the rim of a tall highball glass with the 1/4 lime and dip it into a bowl of coarse salt to coat it lightly. Fill glass with ice and squeeze remaining lime juice into it. Add Jose Cuervo Especial and stir. Fill with tonic water. Garnish with lime slices.

CUERVO ALEXANDER

1 oz. Jose Cuervo gold tequila
1 oz. DeKuyper coffee liqueur
1 oz. DeKuyper cherry brandy
2 scoops vanilla ice cream

Blend until smooth.

CUERVO COOLER

2 parts Jose Cuervo Especial
2 parts Cuarenta y Tres (Licor 43)
seltzer or club soda

Fill a rocks glass 3/4 full of ice cubes, stir together tequila and Licor 43. Top off with seltzer or club soda. Stir well.

CUERVO DREAM

2 parts Jose Cuervo Especial
1 1/2 parts Martini & Rossi dry vermouth
1 1/2 parts Martini & Rossi Rosso vermouth
maraschino cherry

Pour Jose Cuervo Especial and the vermouths into a cock-tail shaker with ice cubes. Shake well. Strain into a chilled martini glass. Garnish with a maraschino cherry.

CUERVO FRESCA

2 parts Jose Cuervo Especial
lemonade
grapefruit
lime
slice of melon
few raspberries

Shake all ingredients (except lemonade) in a cocktail shaker and strain over fresh ice into a rocks glass. Top with lemonade. This works with almost any fruit, herb, or vegetable. Try honey and basil or port and blackberries.

CUERVO MOJITO

2 parts Jose Cuervo Especial
8 fresh mint leaves
1 1/2 tbs. superfine granulated sugar
1 tbs. lime juice
1/3 cup chilled sparkling water

Using the back of a spoon, crush mint with sugar and lime juice in a rocks glass. Fill half of the glass with ice and add Jose Cuervo Especial. Top off the drink with sparkling water and stir well.

CUERVO SHAKE

3 parts Jose Cuervo Especial
1 tsp. honey
1 egg white
6 dashes orange bitters
juice of one lime
sparkling water
lime slice

Shake all ingredients (except sparkling water and lime slice) in a cocktail shaker. Pour into a chilled rocks glass filled with ice cubes. Finish it off with sparkling water and garnish with a lime slice.

CUERVO SIDE-OUT

1 1/2 oz. Jose Cuervo gold tequila
1 oz. Cointreau
2 oz. cranberry juice
1 1/2 oz. lime juice

Blend.

CUERVO STINGER

2 parts Jose Cuervo Especial
2 parts DeKuyper crème de menthe (white)

Pour Jose Cuervo Especial and crème de menthe into a mixing glass with ice cubes. Shake well. Strain into a chilled martini glass.

CUERVO SUNRISE

1 1/2 oz. Jose Cuervo gold tequila
3 oz. cranberry juice
1/2 oz. lime juice
1/2 oz. Rose's grenadine

Shake and serve over ice. Garnish with a lime.

CUERVO SUNRISE II

2 parts Jose Cuervo Especial
2 parts Rose's grenadine
orange juice
pineapple wedge

Pour Jose Cuervo Especial into a chilled tall highball glass over ice. Fill the glass with orange juice leaving a little room on top and stir. Slowly pour in the grenadine. Garnish with a pineapple wedge.

CUERVO TEQUINI

3 parts Jose Cuervo Especial
1/2 part Martini & Rossi dry vermouth
dash Angostura bitters

Garnish with a lemon twist.

CUERVO TROPICAL

1 1/2 oz. Jose Cuervo gold tequila
3 oz. orange juice
1 tsp. lemon juice
1/2 oz. Rose's grenadine

Mix in highball glass filled with cracked ice. Garnish with half an orange slice and a maraschino cherry.

CUERVOPOLITAN

1 1/4 oz. Cuervo Añejo tequila
1/4 oz. Cointreau
1/2 oz. cranberry juice
juice of 1/2 lime

Pour all ingredients into a shaker filled with ice and stir vigorously. Strain into a chilled martini glass.

DEEP RAZZY

6 oz. Bacardi Razz
1 oz. Cointreau
1 oz. Chambord
1 oz. sweet & sour mix
1/2 oz. fresh lime juice

Shake and strain all ingredients into a chilled 10 oz. martini glass. Garnish with three skewered raspberries and a fresh sprig of mint.

DEEP SEA MARTINI

1 1/2 oz. Bombay Sapphire gin
1 oz. Martini & Rossi dry vermouth
dash orange bitters
1/4 oz. Pernod

Stir with ice, strain into a martini glass. Garnish with a lemon peel.

DEPTH CHARGE MARTINI

1 1/4 oz. Bombay Sapphire gin
1 1/4 oz. Lillet
1/4 oz. Pernod
orange peel

Stir with ice, strain into martini glass.

DEWAR'S SIDECAR

1 1/2 oz. Dewar's White Label blended scotch whisky
1/2 oz. Cointreau
1 oz. sweet & sour mix

Optional garnish: maraschino cherry or orange peel.

DEWAR'S & SEVEN NATIONS

2 oz. Dewar's White Label whiskey
fill lemon-lime soda

Serve in a highball glass over ice.

DEWAR'S 12 AND CRANBERRY*

2 oz. Dewar's 12-Year-Old whiskey

Serve neat.

*Note: Cranberries should never be mixed with Dewar's 12, as they would mar the robust, full flavor. Please use cranberries responsibly and bake in muffins or fruitcake, where they belong.

DEWAR'S 12 AND SODA

2 oz. Dewar's 12-Year-Old whiskey
splash soda

DEWAR'S 12 AND WATER

2 oz. Dewar's 12-Year-Old whiskey

Serve in an old-fashioned glass over ice with a splash of water.

DEWAR'S 12 ESKIMO KISS*

2 oz. Dewar's 12-Year-Old whiskey

Serve over ice with a splash of soda.

*Given the typical response when a host receives the thoughtful and elegant gift of Dewar's 12 Year Old, mistletoe may not be required.

DEWAR'S 12 MANHATTAN

1 1/2 oz. Dewar's 12-Year-Old whiskey
1/2 oz. Martini & Rossi Rosso vermouth
dash aromatic bitters

Chill all ingredients in a cocktail shaker; strain and serve straight up in a chilled martini glass. Optional: garnish with cherry or twist of lemon.

DEWAR'S 12 NEAT

2 oz. Dewar's 12-Year-Old whiskey

Serve neat. The only deluxe 12-year-old blended scotch whisky to win Double Gold two years in a row, at the San Francisco World Spirits Competition.

DEWAR'S 12 PEPPERMINT TWIST*

2 oz. Dewar's 12-Year-Old whiskey

Serve over ice with a splash of water.

*Distract fidgety family members with candy canes to ensure serenity while you enjoy your Dewar's 12.

DEWAR'S 12 ROCKS

At 86 Proof, Dewar's 12 stands up to ice better than most deluxes. Pour 2 oz. of Dewar's 12 in a glass, fill it up with ice and enjoy its smooth, full flavor.

DEWAR'S 12 RUSTY NAIL

1 1/2 oz. Dewar's 12-Year-Old whiskey
1/2 oz. Drambuie

Serve in an old-fashioned glass over ice.

DEWAR'S DRY ROB ROY

3 parts Dewar's White Label whiskey
1 part Martini & Rossi dry vermouth

Stir and serve on the rocks or straight up. Add a twist of lemon.

DEWAR'S HIGHBALL

2 oz. Dewar's White Label whiskey
fill ginger ale

Serve in a highball glass over ice and garnish with an orange or lime.

DEWAR'S HIGHLANDER

2 oz. Dewar's White Label whiskey
juice of 1/2 lime

Serve in a highball glass over ice.

DEWAR'S MANHATTAN

1 1/2 oz. Dewar's White Label whiskey
1/2 oz. Martini & Rossi Rosso vermouth
dash aromatic bitters

Chill all ingredients in a cocktail shaker; strain and serve straight up in a chilled martini glass. Optional: garnish with cherry or twist of lemon.

DEWAR'S OLD-FASHIONED

2 1/2 oz. Dewar's White Label whiskey
1/4 tsp. sugar
2 dashes Angostura bitters

Muddle cherry and orange slice in the bottom of an old-fashioned glass. Add ingredients and stir well. Top with club soda or water.

DEWAR'S PERFECT ROB ROY

3 parts Dewar's White Label whiskey
1 part Martini & Rossi Rosso vermouth
1 part Martini & Rossi dry vermouth

Stir and serve on the rocks or straight up. Add cherry or a twist.

DEWAR'S ROB ROY

3 parts Dewar's White Label whiskey
2 parts Martini & Rossi Rosso vermouth

Stir and serve on the rocks or straight up. Add cherry or a twist.

DEWAR'S ROCKS

2 oz. Dewar's White Label whiskey

Serve in an old-fashioned glass over ice.

DEWAR'S RUSTY NAIL

1 1/2 oz. Dewar's White Label whiskey
1/2 oz. Drambuie

Serve in an old-fashioned glass over ice.

DEWAR'S SLING

Dewar's White Label whiskey
sugar syrup
lemon juice
water

Serve over ice in a rocks glass.

DEWAR'S SOUR

2 oz. Dewar's White Label whiskey
1 1/2 oz. sweet & sour mix

Serve in a highball or rocks glass over ice.

DEWAR'S SPLASH

2 oz. Dewar's White Label whiskey

Serve in an old-fashioned glass with a splash of water.

DEWAR'S TWIST

1 1/4 oz. Dewar's White Label whiskey
splash water

Serve in a rocks glass with ice. Garnish with a lemon twist.

DEWEY MARTINI

1 1/2 oz. Vox vodka
dash Martini & Rossi extra dry vermouth
dash orange bitters

Shake and strain into a cocktail glass or serve over ice.

DIABLO

2 parts Jose Cuervo Especial
dash Chambord
ginger beer
lime slice

Pour Jose Cuervo Especial in a tall highball glass full of ice, leaving a little room on top. Add a dash of Chambord. Top off the drink with ginger beer. Garnish with a lime.

DIAMONDS ARE FOREVER

2 1/2 oz. Bombay Sapphire gin
splash Dewar's White Label whiskey

Pour Bombay Sapphire gin and Dewar's over ice and stir. Strain into a well-chilled martini glass. Garnish with olives.

DIMON SHOOTER

1/2 oz. Disaronno amaretto
1/2 oz. Bacardi Limón

Pour into a shot glass. Top off with lemon-lime soda.

DINGLE DRAM

1 1/2 oz. Tullamore Dew Irish whiskey
1/2 oz. Irish Mist
coffee soda
dash DeKuyper crème de cacao
whipped cream

Pour Tullamore Dew Irish whiskey and Irish Mist into a chilled highball glass along with several ice cubes. Fill with coffee soda. Stir gently. Add a float of crème de cacao. Top with a dollop of whipped cream.

DIRTY COOKIE

2/3 shot Carolans Irish cream
1/3 shot DeKuyper green crème de menthe

Shake with ice and strain into a shot glass.

DIRTY DRIFT

1 oz. Drambuie
1 oz. DeKuyper anisette

Serve as a shot or over ice.

DIRTY HARRY

1 oz. Cointreau
1 oz. Tia Maria

Shake with ice and strain.

DIRTY JOB

1 oz. Vox vodka
1 oz. Cointreau
tonic water

Pour Vox vodka and Cointreau into a tumbler glass full of ice. Fill with tonic water and stir.

DIRTY NELLY

1 oz. Carolans Irish cream
1 oz. Tullamore Dew Irish whiskey

Shake.

DISARITA MARGARITA

1 oz. Jose Cuervo 1800 tequila
1/2 oz. Disaronno amaretto
3 oz. margarita mix
1/2 cup crushed ice

Blend.

DISARITA

1 oz. Jose Cuervo 1800 tequila
1/2 oz. Disaronno amaretto
3 oz. margarita mix
1/2 cup crushed ice

Blend. Garnish with a lime.

DISARONNO ALEXANDER

1 oz. Disaronno amaretto
1 oz. DeKuyper crème de cacao
1 oz. cream

Shake all ingredients with ice, strain into a cocktail glass, and serve.

DISARONNO AND CREAM

2 oz. Disaronno amaretto
1 oz. cream or milk

Pour Disaronno and cream over ice. Stir and serve in an old-fashioned glass.

DISARONNO BOCCE BALL

2 oz. Disaronno amaretto
6 oz. chilled orange juice
splash soda
lime slice, optional

Pour Disaronno and orange juice in a glass over ice. Add a splash of soda. Stir and garnish with a lime slice.

DISARONNO CAPPUCcINO

1 1/2 oz. Disaronno amaretto
6 oz. cappuccino

Pour Disaronno into hot cappuccino and serve.

DISARONNO CHERRY BOMB

2 oz. Disaronno amaretto
4 oz. cola or diet cola

Serve in a rocks glass over ice. Garnish with a maraschino cherry.

DISARONNO COSMOPOLITAN

1 oz. Disaronno amaretto
1 oz. Bacardi Limón
splash cranberry juice

Stir with ice and strain into a martini glass.

DISARONNO HOT CHOCOLATE

2 oz. Disaronno amaretto
6 oz. hot chocolate

In a mug, pour Disaronno liqueur into hot chocolate. Top with whipped cream.

DISARONNO ITALIAN TICKLER

2 oz. Disaronno amaretto
5 oz. club soda

DISARONNO MARGARITA

1 oz. Disaronno amaretto
3 oz. margarita mix
1 oz. Jose Cuervo tequila

Shake well with ice and strain into a salt-rimmed glass. Garnish with a lime slice.

DISARONNO MIMOSA

1/2 cup Disaronno amaretto
3 cups orange juice
750-ml bottle chilled Martini & Rossi Asti sparkling wine

In a pitcher, stir together orange juice and Disaronno. Fill each of six champagne flutes halfway with juice mixture and top off with sparkling wine. Makes about twelve drinks.

DISARONNO PUNCH

1 1/2 oz. Disaronno amaretto
1 oz. Bacardi Limón
3 oz. cranberry juice

Serve over ice.

DISARONNO ROYALE

1 oz. Disaronno amaretto
champagne

Pour Disaronno into a chilled champagne flute. Top off with champagne.

DISARONNO SOUR

2 oz. Disaronno amaretto
4 oz. sweet & sour mix

Combine ingredients with cracked ice in a cocktail shaker. Shake well and strain into chilled, sugar-rimmed glass over ice cubes.

DISARONNO SUNRISE

1 1/2 oz. Disaronno amaretto
1 oz. Bacardi rum
3 oz. orange juice

Serve over ice in a tall glass.

DISARONNO TICKLER

2 oz. Disaronno amaretto
5 oz. club soda

Mix with ice. Serve in a tall glass.

DISARONNO TOASTED ALMOND

1 1/2 oz. Disaronno amaretto
1 oz. cream
1 oz. DeKuyper coffee liqueur

Pour Disaronno and DeKuyper coffee liqueur into an old-fashioned glass over ice. Float cream or milk on top by pouring it in gently over the back of a teaspoon.

DISARTINI

1 oz. Disaronno amaretto
1 oz. Bombay Sapphire gin

Stir (do not shake) with ice and strain into chilled martini glass. Garnish with a twist of orange rind.

DISCO

1 1/2 oz. mango-infused Vox vodka
1/2 oz. Chambord
2 oz. cranberry juice

Shake and pour over ice and garnish with a chocolate disc.

DIXIE DEW

1 1/2 oz. Knob Creek bourbon
1/2 oz. DeKuyper white crème de menthe
1/2 tsp. Cointreau

Combine all of the ingredients in a mixing glass half-filled with ice cubes. Stir well. Strain into a cocktail glass.

DIXIE JULEP

1 tsp. powdered sugar
2 oz. Knob Creek bourbon

Put sugar and bourbon into a collins glass. Fill with crushed ice and stir gently. Decorate with sprigs of mint.

DIXIE STINGER

3 oz. Knob Creek bourbon
1/2 oz. DeKuyper white crème de menthe
1/2 tsp. Southern Comfort

In a shaker half-filled with ice cubes, combine all of the ingredients. Shake well. Strain into a cocktail glass.

DIXIE WHISKEY COCKTAIL

2 oz. Knob Creek bourbon
1/2 tsp. DeKuyper white crème de menthe
1/4 tsp. Cointreau
1/2 tsp. powdered sugar
dash bitters

Shake with ice and strain into a cocktail glass.

DIZZY LIZZY

1 1/2 oz. Knob Creek bourbon
1 1/2 oz. Sherry
dash lemon juice
club soda

*Combine first three ingredients in a tall glass with ice.
Fill with club soda.*

DOUBLE GOLD

1/2 oz. Jose Cuervo gold tequila
1/2 oz. Goldschlager

Shake with ice and strain into a shot glass.

DRAMBUIE AFTER

*After dining, pour Drambuie into a cordial glass and
serve neat.*

DRAMBUIE CIDER

*Add 2 oz. Drambuie to hot apple cider. Add a stick of cin-
namon.*

DRAMBUIE COFFEE

*Serve freshly brewed coffee lightly sweetened with
Drambuie in a warm glass. Top with fresh cream. Equally
pleasing when served with hot tea instead of coffee.*

DRAMBUIE MIST

Pour Drambuie over crushed ice and add a lemon twist.

DRAMBUIE ON ICE

A generous measure of Drambuie poured over ice. An after dinner delight.

DREAM COCKTAIL

2 oz. Hennessy cognac
1/2 oz. Cointreau
1 tsp. DeKuyper anisette

Shake with ice and strain into a cocktail glass.

DUBLIN COFFEE

1 oz. DeKuyper coffee liqueur
1/2 oz. Irish Mist hot coffee
whipped cream

Serve in a coffee mug.

DUBLIN HANDSHAKE

1/2 oz. Carolans Irish cream
1/2 oz. Tullamore Dew Irish whiskey
3/4 oz. Bombay Sapphire gin

Shake with crushed ice. Strain into a cocktail glass.

DUBONNET COCKTAIL

1 1/2 oz. Dubonnet
1/2 oz. Bombay Sapphire gin
dash Angostura bitters

Combine over ice.

DUCK PIN

1 oz. Chambord
1 oz. Southern Comfort
1/2 oz. pineapple juice

Shake with ice and strain into a shot glass.

DUNDEE

2 tsp. Drambuie
1 1/2 oz. Bombay dry gin
2 tbs. Dewar's scotch
1 tsp. lemon juice

Fill mixing glass with ice, add Bombay, Dewar's, Drambuie, and lemon juice. Shake, strain into a rocks glass, and add ice. Garnish with a maraschino cherry and a lemon twist.

EAST INDIA

1 1/2 oz. Hennessy cognac
1/2 oz. Cointreau
1/2 oz. pineapple juice
dash Angostura bitters

Shake and strain into a martini or wine glass.

ELECTRIC PEACH

1 oz. Vox vodka
1/4 oz. DeKuyper Peachtree schnapps
1/2 oz. cranberry juice cocktail
1/4 oz. orange juice

Blend. Garnish with a lemon slice.

ELECTRIC SCREWDRIVER

1 part Jose Cuervo Especial
1 part Vox vodka
4 parts orange juice
lemon slice

Mix Jose Cuervo Especial, vodka, and orange juice in a chilled tall highball glass over ice. Garnish with a lemon slice.

ELECTRIC TICKLER

1/4 oz. Drambuie
1 1/2 oz. Bombay dry gin
1/4 oz. Martini & Rossi Rosso vermouth
orange juice
club soda

In a collins glass, shake with ice, strain over ice. Fill with soda. Lemon garnish.

ELEGANT MARTINI BOMBAY SAPPHIRE GIN

1 3/4 oz. Bombay Sapphire gin
1/2 oz. Martini & Rossi dry vermouth
1/4 oz. Cointreau
dash Cointreau (on top)

Stir the first three ingredients with ice. Strain or serve on ice. Float Cointreau on top.

ELEGANT MARTINI VOX VODKA

1 1/2 oz. Vox vodka
dash Martini & Rossi extra dry vermouth
1/4 oz. Cointreau
dash Cointreau (on top)

Stir the first three ingredients with ice. Serve on ice or straight up. Cointreau on top.

ELIXIR OF LOVE

1 1/2 oz. Disaronno amaretto
1/2 oz. DeKuyper crème de cacao
1/2 oz. Bacardi light rum
2 oz. cream

Serve over crushed ice.

EMERALD ISLE

3/4 shot Tullamore Dew
3/4 shot DeKuyper green crème de menthe
2 scoops vanilla ice cream
soda water

Blend first three ingredients then add soda water. Stir after adding soda water.

ERIE TOUR

1/3 Irish Mist
1/3 Carolans Irish cream
1/3 Tullamore Dew Irish whiskey

Serve over ice.

ERIN GO BURRR

3 oz. Carolans Irish cream

Serve chilled Carolans Irish cream straight up in a chilled cocktail glass.

EVERYTHING

1 oz. Bombay Sapphire gin
1/2 oz. Martini & Rossi extra dry vermouth
1/2 oz. Martini & Rossi Rosso vermouth
dash DeKuyper white crème de menthe
2 dashes bitters

Stir on the rocks.

EYES R SMILIN'

1 oz. Carolans Irish cream
1 oz. Vox vodka
1/2 oz. Bombay Sapphire gin
1/2 oz. Cointreau

Build over ice. Stir and serve.

FALLEN ANGEL

1/2 oz. Bombay Sapphire gin
1/2 oz. DeKuyper apricot brandy
1/4 oz. brandy

Shake. Serve straight up.

FAT CAT

1 oz. Hennessy cognac
3/4 oz. Galliano
1/4 oz. DeKuyper white crème de cacao
1 cup vanilla ice cream

Blend until smooth. Pour into a wine goblet.

FEMME FATALE

2 oz. Hennessy VS
2 oz. cranberry juice

Combine in a snifter and fill with Moet & Chandon Nectar Imperial. Add rocks.

FOG CUTTER

1/2 oz. Bombay Sapphire gin
1 1/2 oz. Bacardi light rum
1/2 oz. brandy
1 oz. orange juice
3 tbs. lemon juice

Shake all ingredients and strain into a collins glass with ice.

FOGGY DAY MARTINI

1 1/2 oz. Bombay Sapphire gin
1/4 oz. Pernod
twist lemon peel

Shake and pour over ice or serve straight up. Garnish with a lemon twist.

FOOL'S GOLD

1 part Vox vodka
1 part Galliano

Shake with ice and strain into a shot glass.

FORBIDDEN FRUIT

1/2 oz. DeKuyper Pucker sour apple
1/2 oz. DeKuyper Peachtree schnapps
1/2 oz. Knob Creek bourbon
1 1/2 oz. sweet & sour mix

Shake with ice and serve over ice.

FOURTH DEGREE MARTINI

3/4 oz. Bombay Sapphire gin
3/4 oz. Martini & Rossi dry vermouth
3/4 oz. Martini & Rossi Rosso vermouth
1/4 oz. Pernod

Garnish with a lemon peel twist. Stir gently with ice; serve straight up or over ice.

FOURTH OF JULY

1/3 shot Rose's grenadine
1/3 shot Vox vodka
1/3 shot DeKuyper blue curacao

Layer this drink in the order listed.

FREDDIE FUDPUCKER

1 oz. Jose Cuervo tequila
4 oz. orange juice
1/2 oz. Galliano
1/2 oz. DeKuyper coffee liqueur

Shake and serve over ice.

FRENCH COLADA

1 1/2 oz. Bacardi light rum
3/4 oz. Hennessy cognac
1 scoop crushed ice
3/4 oz. sweet cream
3/4 oz. Coco Lopez cream of coconut
1 1/2 oz. pineapple juice
splash DeKuyper crème de cassis

Blend.

FRENCH CREAM

1 1/2 oz. Carolans Irish cream
1/2 oz. Chambord
2 oz. half-and-half
4 oz. ice cubes

Blend.

FRENCH KISS

2 parts Vox vodka
1 1/2 parts Chambord
3/4 part DeKuyper white crème de cacao
3/4 part cream

Shake ingredients with ice and strain into a glass.

FRENCH MARTINI

1/2 oz. Chambord
1 1/2 oz. Vox vodka
2 oz. pineapple juice

Shake and pour over ice.

FRENCH SUMMER

1/4 oz. Chambord
3 oz. sparkling water
slice lemon and orange

Pour the Chambord into a wine glass filled with ice. Add the sparkling water and the juice of a slice of lemon and orange. Stir.

FRENCH "75"

1 1/2 oz. Bombay Sapphire gin
2 tsp. superfine sugar
1 1/2 oz. lemon juice
4 oz. champagne, chilled
1 maraschino cherry

Shake well, except champagne. Pour into a collins glass. Top with champagne. Stir well and garnish with a maraschino cherry.

FRU-FRU

3/4 oz. DeKuyper crème de banana liqueur
1 oz. DeKuyper Peachtree schnapps
dash Rose's lime juice
1 oz. pineapple juice

Shake with ice and strain into a shot glass.

FRUIT BLAST MARTINI COCKTAIL

1 oz. Bacardi O
1 oz. Bacardi Tropico
1 1/2 oz. pineapple juice
1 oz. cranberry juice

Shake with ice; strain into martini glass and garnish with a strawberry.

FRUIT COCKTAIL

1/2 oz. each of DeKuyper Pucker Cheri-Beri and grape schnapps.

Serve as a shot or on the rocks.

FRUIT SALAD

Equal parts (1/2 oz. each):
    DeKuyper Pucker Cheri-Beri
    DeKuyper Pucker grape schanpps
    DeKuyper Peachtree schnapps
splash of orange juice

Combine; serve as shot or over ice.

FRUIT SALAD II

Equal parts:
    DeKuyper Pucker sour apple
    DeKuyper Pucker Cheri-Beri
    DeKuyper Pucker grape schnapps
splash orange juice

Combine; serve as shot or over ice.

FRUIT SALAD SLAMMER

Equal parts:
    DeKuyper Pucker sour apple
    DeKuyper Pucker grape schnapps
    DeKuyper Pucker Cheri-Beri

Mix equal parts, chill and serve in a shot glass.

FRUITY IRISHMAN

2 parts Carolans Irish cream
1 part DeKuyper melon liqueur

Stir.

FUDGESICLE

1 oz. Vox vodka
1/4 oz. DeKuyper crème de cacao
1/4 oz. chocolate syrup

Shake and serve over ice.

FUN AT THE BEACH

1 oz. DeKuyper Peachtree schnapps
1 oz. DeKuyper Pucker sour apple
3 oz. cranberry juice
3 oz. pineapple juice

Serve over ice in a tall glass.

FUZZ BALL

1 oz. DeKuyper Pucker watermelon schnapps
1 oz. DeKuyper Peachtree schnapps

Serve in a shot glass.

FUZZY NAVEL

1 1/4 oz. DeKuyper Peachtree schnapps
3 oz. orange juice

Pour schnapps over ice in a rocks glass. Fill with orange juice and stir well.

FUZZY RITA

1/2 oz. Cointreau
1 1/2 oz. Jose Cuervo tequila
1/2 oz. DeKuyper Peachtree schnapps
1 1/2 oz. lime juice

Combine over ice in a tall glass.

GASSER

1 oz. Drambuie
1 1/2 oz. Dewar's scotch
1 tbs. Martini & Rossi Rosso vermouth
2 dashes orange bitters

In an old-fashioned glass, shake with ice, strain over ice. Add an orange twist.

GENTLEMAN'S COCKTAIL

1 1/2 oz. Knob Creek bourbon
1/2 oz. Hennessy cognac
1/2 oz. DeKuyper white crème de menthe
club soda

Pour bourbon, Hennessy, and crème de menthe over ice into highball glass. Add club soda and garnish with a lemon wheel.

GIBSON

2 oz. Bombay dry gin
dash Martini & Rossi extra dry vermouth
cocktail onion

Stir with ice. Add the cocktail onion. Serve straight up or on ice.

GIMLET

1 1/4 oz. Vox vodka
1/2 oz. fresh lime juice

Mix Vox vodka and lime juice in a glass with ice. Strain and serve in a cocktail glass. Garnish with a lime twist.

GIMLET II

2 oz. Bombay Sapphire gin
1/2 oz. Martini & Rossi extra dry vermouth
1/2 oz. Rose's lime juice
1 lime slice

Serve over ice.

GLOWLIGHT

1/2 oz. Drambuie
1 1/2 oz. Bombay dry gin
1/2 oz. Jose Cuervo tequila
1 tsp. grenadine
1/2 tsp. Bacardi light rum
club soda
2 maraschino cherries

In a collins glass, pour over ice, fill with soda. Add grenadine and maraschino cherries. Float Bacardi.

GODCHILD

1 oz. Disaronno amaretto
1 oz. Vox vodka
1 oz. cream or half-and-half

Shake with ice. Strain into a chilled martini glass.

GODFATHER

1 oz. Disaronno amaretto
1 oz. Dewar's White Label whiskey

Pour over ice in a rocks glass.

GODMOTHER

1 oz. Disaronno amaretto
1 oz. Vox vodka

Pour over ice in a rocks glass.

GOLD DIGGER MARTINI

1/2 oz. Cointreau
1 oz. Vox vodka
1/2 oz. pineapple juice

Stir with ice; serve straight up or over ice.

GOLDEN BOY

1 1/2 oz. Knob Creek bourbon
1/2 oz. Bacardi rum
2 oz. orange juice
1 tsp. lemon juice
1 tsp. sugar syrup
1 scoop crushed ice
dash Rose's grenadine

Mix all ingredients, except the Rose's grenadine, in a shaker. Strain mixture into a chilled glass. Top with a dash of Rose's grenadine.

GOLDEN CADILLAC

1/4 oz. Galliano
1 oz. DeKuyper white crème de cacao
1 oz. cream

Mix in a blender with a little ice. Strain into a champagne glass. A scoop of vanilla ice cream may be substituted for cream.

GOLDEN DAY

3/4 oz. Vox vodka
1/2 oz. Liquore Galliano

Serve in a rocks glass over ice.

GOLDEN GIRL MARTINI

1 3/4 oz. Bombay Sapphire gin
3/4 oz. dry Sherry
dash Angostura bitters

Stir and strain into a martini glass.

GOLDEN PEACH

3/4 oz. DeKuyper Peachtree schnapps
1 oz. Bombay Sapphire gin
5 oz. orange juice

In a tall glass with ice, fill with orange juice, and stir well.

GOLDEN DREAM

1/2 oz. Cointreau
1 oz. Liquore Galliano
1/2 oz. orange juice
1/2 oz. cream

Shake with cracked ice. Strain into a cocktail glass. You can also serve this over ice in a highball glass.

GOOD AND PLENTY

1 oz. DeKuyper anisette
1 oz. DeKuyper blackberry brandy

Shake with ice and strain into a shot glass.

GOTHAM BAR & GRILL AVIATION

3 1/2 oz. Bombay Sapphire gin
1 1/2 oz. maraschino liqueur
juice of 1/2 lemon

Mix all ingredients with cracked ice in shaker; strain into a martini glass. Garnish with a cherry.

The Gotham Bar & Grill
New York City, NY

GRAND CENTRAL MARTINI

3 oz. Bombay Sapphire gin
3 squirts sauce
small squirt lemon juice
1 blue point oyster, shucked

Mix all ingredients with cracked ice in shaker; strain into a martini glass. Garnish with an oyster.

The Grand Central Oyster Bar
Grand Central Station
New York City, NY

GRAND MARGARITA

1 oz. Jose Cuervo tequila
3/4 oz. Cointreau
fresh lime juice
sugar

Fill shaker with ice. Add Cuervo and the Cointreau. Fill with lime juice and add sugar to taste. Shake. Pour over ice or strain. Garnish with a lime wedge.

GRAPE & CHERI-BERI SNOW CONES

1 oz. DeKuyper Pucker grape schnapps
1 oz. Dekuyper Cheri-Beri Pucker

Serve over crushed ice.

GRAPPLER

3/4 oz. DeKuyper Pucker sour apple
3/4 oz. DeKuyper Pucker grape schnapps
soda water

Serve over ice.

GRASSHOPPER

1/2 oz. DeKuyper green crème de menthe
1/2 oz. DeKuyper white crème de cacao
1/2 oz. cream

Blend and serve in a wine glass.

GREEN HORNET

1/2 oz. Vox vodka
1/4 oz. DeKuyper melon liqueur
1/2 oz. sweet & sour mix

Shake with ice; serve straight up or over ice.

GREEN LIZARD

1 part Chartreuse
1 part Bacardi 151 rum
1 part Rose's lime juice

Layer this drink by pouring Chartreuse first, then the rum, and then the lime juice.

GREEN MONDAY

1 1/2 oz. Cointreau
mint leaves
lemon-lime soda

Fill a tumbler glass with crushed ice and mint leaves. Pour Cointreau over ice and fill with lemon-lime soda.

GREEN SNEAKER

1 oz. Vox vodka
1/2 oz. DeKuyper melon liqueur
1/2 oz. Cointreau
2 oz. orange juice

Stir with ice, strain, and serve straight up.

GREMLIN

1 1/2 oz. Vox vodka
3/4 oz. DeKuyper blue curacao
3/4 oz. Bacardi rum
1/2 oz. orange juice

Shake with ice, strain, and serve straight up.

GREYHOUND

1 1/2 oz. Vox vodka
grapefruit juice

Pour Vox vodka over crushed ice in a tall glass. Fill with grapefruit juice.

GREYHOUND MARTINI

2 parts Vox vodka
4 parts grapefruit juice

Shake ingredients with ice and strain into a glass.

GRIT COCKTAIL

1 oz. Tullamore Dew Irish whiskey
1 oz. Martini & Rossi dry vermouth

Shake and then strain into a shot glass or serve over ice.

GUNRUNNER

1/2 oz. Drambuie
1/2 oz. Dewar's scotch
1 1/2 oz. Disaronno amaretto
1 tbs. Bacardi rum

Shake with ice and strain over ice in a tall glass.

GUNGA DIN MARTINI

3 parts Bombay Sapphire gin
1 part Martini & Rossi dry vermouth
juice of 1/4 orange

Shake with ice. Garnish with a pineapple slice.

GYPSY MARTINI

1 1/2 oz. Vox vodka or Bombay Sapphire gin
dash Martini & Rossi extra dry vermouth

*Shake with ice; serve straight up or on ice. Garnish with
a maraschino cherry.*

GYPSY'S KISS

1 part Irish Mist
1 part orange juice
1 part lemon juice or sweet & sour mix

Combine in a highball glass. You can also add a dash of Rose's grenadine.

HALF-AND-HALF MARTINI

3 parts Bombay Sapphire gin
3 parts Vox vodka
1 part Martini & Rossi dry vermouth

Shake with ice; serve straight up or on ice. Garnish with a lemon twist.

HARD HAT

1 1/4 oz. Bacardi rum
1 1/4 oz. fresh lime juice
1 tsp. sugar
1/4 oz. Rose's grenadine
club soda

In a shaker with ice, combine all but the club soda. Stir and strain into a glass with ice. Fill with club soda.

HARVARD COCKTAIL

2 oz. Hennessy cognac
1 oz. Martini & Rossi Rosso vermouth
1 oz. lemon juice
1 tsp. Rose's grenadine
dash bitters

Shake with ice and strain into a cocktail glass.

HARVEY WALLBANGER

1/4 oz. Liquore Galliano
1 oz. Vox vodka
orange juice

In a tall glass with ice, add Vox vodka and fill the glass with orange juice. Float the Galliano on top.

HAVANA SIDECAR

1 1/2 oz. Bacardi rum
3/4 oz. lemon juice
3/4 oz. Cointreau

Mix with ice and serve on ice.

HAWAIIAN COCKTAIL MARTINI

2 oz. Bombay Sapphire gin
1/2 oz. Cointreau
1/2 oz. unsweetened pineapple juice

Shake and strain.

HAWAIIAN NIGHT

1 oz. Bacardi light rum
1/4 oz. DeKuyper cherry brandy
pineapple juice

Pour rum into a tall glass half filled with ice. Fill with pineapple juice and float cherry brandy on top.

HAZELNUT COFFEE

B & B and hazelnut liqueur with coffee and whipped cream.

HENNESSY CONTINENTAL

1 oz. Hennessy cognac
splash Cointreau
1 1/2 oz. cranberry juice
1/2 oz. grapefruit juice

Strain into a chilled martini glass.

HENNESSY CHOCOLATE MARTINI

2 oz. Hennessy cognac
1 oz. DeKuyper crème de cacao

Shake with ice.

HENNESSY SOUR

1 oz. Hennessy V.S
1 oz. sweet & sour mix

Shake with ice. Pour into a snifter glass.

HIGH VOLTAGE

1/2 oz. lime or lemon juice
1/2 oz. Cointreau
1 oz. Dewar's scotch

Pour lime or lemon juice, Cointreau, and Dewar's into an old-fashioned glass with ice. Fill with soda water. Stir.

HOME RUN

1 oz. Knob Creek bourbon
1/2 oz. Bacardi light rum
1 oz. Hennessy cognac
2 tsp. lemon juice

Shake with ice and serve over ice.

HONOLULU HURRICANE MARTINI

4 parts Bombay Sapphire gin
1 part Martini & Rossi dry vermouth
1 part Martini & Rossi Rosso vermouth
1 tsp. pineapple juice

Shake and strain into a martini glass.

HOP-SKIP-AND-GO NAKED

1 oz. Vox vodka
1 oz. Bombay Sapphire gin
juice of 1/2 lime

Serve in a mug over ice. Fill with Budweiser.

HORNY BULL

1 1/4 oz. Jose Cuervo tequila
orange juice

Add Cuervo to a chilled highball glass filled with ice. Fill with orange juice.

HORSESHOT

1 1/4 oz. Vox vodka
4 oz. tomato juice
1 1/4 tsp. horseradish

Serve over ice in a cocktail glass. Garnish with a celery stalk or tomato slice.

HOT APPLE

3 oz. Laird's applejack
3 oz. hot cider or apple juice

Pour into a thick tumbler or mug. Twist and drop in a spiral of lemon peel, dust with powdered cinnamon or a cinnamon stick.

HOT APPLE PIE

3/4 oz. DeKuyper Pucker sour apple
1/4 oz. DeKuyper Hot Damn!

Fill with hot apple cider; garnish with a cinnamon stick.

HOT APPLE RUM

3/4 oz. DeKuyper Pucker sour apple
3/4 oz. Bacardi rum
5 oz. hot water
2 tsp. butter

Sprinkle with cinnamon and serve in a mug.

HOT APPLE TODDY

3/4 oz. DeKuyper Pucker sour apple
3/4 oz. DeKuyper Thrilla Vanilla
6 oz. hot apple cider/juice

Serve in a mug.

HOT BUTTERED COMFORT

1 jigger Southern Comfort
small cinnamon stick
slice lemon peel
pat butter

Float butter. Stir. Serve in a coffee cup or mug.

HOT IRISH

1 1/2 oz. Tullamore Dew Irish whiskey
2 tsp. sugar (brown if available)
1/2 slice fresh lemon
4 cloves
pinch cinnamon

Stud the lemon slice with cloves. Put lemon, sugar, and cinnamon into a warm glass. Add boiling water and Irish whiskey. Stir well and serve in a mug or coffee cup.

HOT MIST

2 parts Irish Mist
1 part boiling water

Combine in the glass and garnish with a slice of lemon and some cloves.

HOT MULLED

2 oz. Dewar's 12-Year-Old whiskey

Serve with a splash of hot water.

HOT TODDY

2 oz. Knob Creek bourbon
1 tsp. sugar

Add boiling water. Serve in a mug. Garnish with a lemon slice and dust with nutmeg or add a cinnamon stick.

HULA HOOP

1 1/2 oz. Vox vodka
2 oz. pineapple juice
1/2 oz. orange juice

Combine over ice.

ILLUSION

1 oz. Cointreau
1/2 oz. Bacardi rum
1/2 oz. DeKuyper melon liqueur
1/2 oz. Vox vodka
2 oz. pineapple juice

Serve in a tall glass with ice.

IMPERIAL

1 1/4 oz. Knob Creek bourbon
splash club soda
1 1/4 oz. Cointreau
splash simple syrup
1 scoop crushed ice

Mix together all the ingredients except the club soda in a shaker. Strain the mixture into a rocks glass over ice. Top off the glass with club soda.

INOCULATION SHOT

1 oz. Jose Cuervo gold tequila
1/4 oz. DeKuyper blue curacao

Shake with ice and strain into a shot glass.

IRISH ANGEL

3/4 oz. Tullamore Dew Irish whiskey
1/4 oz. DeKuyper white crème de cacao
1/4 oz. DeKuyper white crème de menthe
1 1/2 oz. heavy cream

Shake and serve in a martini glass.

IRISH APPLE

2 parts Carolans Irish cream
1 part Laird's applejack

Stir.

IRISH BUCK

1 1/2 oz. Tullamore Dew Irish whiskey
ginger ale

Pour Tullamore Dew Irish whiskey into chilled highball glass with cracked ice. Twist a lemon peel over the drink and drop it in. Fill with ginger ale.

IRISH CANADIAN

1/2 oz. Irish Mist
1 1/2 oz. Canadian whisky

Stir well and serve.

IRISH CELEBRATION

1 1/4 oz. Tullamore Dew Irish whiskey
1/4 oz. DeKuyper green crème de menthe
splash champagne

Shake; top with champagne.

IRISH CHARLIE

1 part Carolans Irish cream
1 part DeKuyper white crème de menthe

Shake with ice and strain into a shot glass. You can also layer the Irish cream over the crème de menthe.

IRISH COFFEE

Into a stemmed glass, put 2 tsp. sugar, preferably brown; add 1/3 Tullamore Dew Irish whiskey and 2/3 really strong black coffee, preferably freshly brewed, not instant. The glass should be filled with this mixture to within half an inch of the brim. Stir well at this point to ensure all of the sugar is dissolved, and then carefully float over the back of a spoon a collar of lightly whipped cream, so that the cream floats on the top of the coffee and whiskey. Do not stir anymore. Serve the drink without a spoon or a straw, as part of the pleasure comes from sipping the hot coffee and whiskey through the cool cream. It's Ray Foley's favorite.

IRISH COFFEE (SIMPLE)

Tullamore Dew Irish whiskey, hot coffee, sugar, whipped cream.

IRISH COOLER

1 1/4 oz. Tullamore Dew
6 oz. club soda

Garnish with a lemon peel spiral.

IRISH COW

1 1/2 oz. Tullamore Dew Irish whiskey
8 oz. hot milk
1 tsp. sugar

Pour the milk into a glass. Add the sugar and whiskey. Stir well.

IRISH COWBOY

1 part Carolans Irish cream
1 part Knob Creek bourbon

Shake and serve over ice.

IRISH CREAM STINGER

3 parts Carolans Irish cream
1 part DeKuyper white crème de menthe

Stir well over ice.

IRISH CUP O' JOE

Carolans Irish cream, chocolate syrup, hot coffee.

IRISH DELIGHT

1 1/2 oz. Tullamore Dew Irish whiskey
3/4 oz. cream

Stir and serve.

IRISH DREAM

1/2 oz. Carolans Irish cream
1/2 oz. DeKuyper hazelnut liqueur
1/2 oz. DeKuyper dark crème de cacao
1 scoop vanilla ice cream

Blend and serve.

IRISH EYES

1 oz. Tullamore Dew Irish whiskey
1/4 oz. DeKuyper green crème de menthe
2 oz. heavy cream

Shake well with crushed ice. Strain into a chilled cocktail glass. Garnish with a maraschino cherry.

IRISH FIX

2 oz. Tullamore Dew Irish whiskey
1/2 oz. Irish Mist
1 oz. pineapple juice
1/2 oz. lemon juice
1/2 tsp. sugar syrup

Fill a mixing glass with ice. Combine ingredients and stir.

IRISH FROST SHOOTER

1 shot Carolans Irish cream
1 splash Coco Lopez cream of coconut
1 splash half-and-half

Shake and strain. Garnish with cinnamon.

IRISH HEADLOCK

1/4 oz. Carolans Irish cream
1/4 oz. Tullamore Dew Irish whiskey
1/4 oz. Disaronno amaretto
1/4 oz. brandy

Layer in above order.

IRISH KISS

3/4 oz. Tullamore Dew Irish whiskey
1/2 oz. DeKuyper Peachtree schnapps
4 oz. ginger ale
2 oz. orange juice

Combine ingredients in an ice cube-filled collins glass. Garnish with a lime wheel.

IRISH KNIGHT

2 oz. Tullamore Dew Irish whiskey
2 oz. Martini & Rossi dry vermouth
2 dashes Benedictine

Combine in a rocks glass with ice. Add a twist of orange peel.

IRISH KNIT

1 oz. Carolans Irish cream
1 oz. Cointreau
hot coffee

Serve in a warm mug.

IRISH LACED

1 shot Irish Mist
2 splashes Coco Lopez cream of coconut
2 splashes half-and-half
3 splashes pineapple juice
2 scoops ice

Blend. Serve in a tall glass.

IRISH MAGIC

1 oz. Tullamore Dew Irish whiskey
1/4 oz. DeKuyper white crème de cacao
5 oz. orange juice

Pour all ingredients over ice in a glass. Stir.

IRISH MIST ALEXANDER

1 oz. Irish Mist
1 oz. light cream
1 oz. DeKuyper dark crème de cacao

Shake ingredients with cracked ice and strain. Sprinkle with nutmeg.

IRISH MIST COFFEE

hot coffee
1 1/2 oz. Irish Mist

Top with whipped cream.

IRISH MIST KISS

1 part Irish Mist
dash DeKuyper blue curacao
splash soda

Serve in a rocks glass over ice.

IRISH MIST SODA

1 part Irish Mist
3 parts club soda

Serve with ice and a wedge of lime or lemon in a tall glass.

IRISH NIGHTCAP

1 1/2 oz. Tullamore Dew Irish whiskey
4 oz. hot milk
1 tsp. sugar

Stir.

IRISH PENANCE

1 part Carolans Irish cream
1 part Cointreau

Shake slowly and serve on the rocks.

IRISH PRINCE

1 1/4 oz. Tullamore Dew Irish whiskey
3 oz. tonic water

Stir.

IRISH RICKEY

1 1/2 oz. Tullamore Dew Irish whiskey
1 cube ice
juice of 1/2 lime

Fill 8 oz. highball glass with carbonated water and stir. Leave lime in glass.

IRISH ROSE HIGHBALL

1 jigger Tullamore Dew Irish whiskey
1/3 jigger Rose's grenadine
club soda

Combine first two ingredients in a glass and fill with club soda.

IRISH RUSSIAN

1 part Carolans Irish cream
1 part Vox vodka

Stir.

IRISH SHILLELAGH

1 1/2 oz. Tullamore Dew Irish whiskey
1/2 oz. DeKuyper sloe gin
1/2 oz. Bacardi light rum
1 oz. lemon juice
1 tsp. sugar syrup
2 peach slices, diced

*Mix all ingredients with cracked ice in a shaker or blend.
Pour into a chilled rocks glass. Garnish with raspberries
and a maraschino cherry.*

IRISH SLING

1 oz. Tullamore Dew Irish whiskey
1 oz. Bombay Sapphire gin
1 lump sugar

*Crush sugar with ice in a glass. Add Tullamore Dew and
gin and stir.*

IRISH SOUR

1 1/2 oz. Tullamore Dew Irish whiskey
1 tsp. sugar
juice of 1/2 lemon

*Shake vigorously with ice until frothy. Stir into a sour
glass. Add a maraschino cherry and an orange slice.*

IRISH SPRING

1 oz. Tullamore Dew Irish whiskey
1/2 oz. DeKuyper Peachtree schnapps
1 oz. orange juice
1 oz. sweet & sour mix

In a collins glass with ice, stir well. Garnish with an orange slice and a maraschino cherry.

IRISH STING

1 1/2 oz. Tullamore Dew Irish whiskey
1/4 oz. DeKuyper white crème de menthe

Shake. Serve straight up or over ice.

IRISH SUMMER COFFEE

1 oz. Tullamore Dew Irish whiskey
1/4 oz. Carolans Irish cream
4 oz. cold coffee
whipped cream

Stir first three ingredients with ice and strain. Top with whipped cream if desired.

IRISH SURFER

1 1/4 oz. Irish Mist
3 oz. orange juice
sugar
club soda

Shake Irish Mist, orange juice, and sugar. Top with club soda.

ISLAND ECSTASY

2 parts DeKuyper tropical pineapple
1 part Vox vodka
splash Rose's grenadine

Fill with orange juice. Serve over ice in a tall glass.

ISLAND TEA

1 1/2 oz. Vox vodka
1 oz. Rose's grenadine
1 tsp. lemon juice

Combine with ice and shake. Strain over ice in a rocks glass and garnish with a mint sprig.

ITALIAN APPLE COFFEE

3/4 oz. DeKuyper Pucker sour apple
3/4 oz. Disaronno amaretto
6 oz. fresh coffee

Serve in a mug.

ITALIAN COLADA

1/4 oz. Coco Lopez cream of coconut
1 1/2 oz. Bacardi light rum
1/4 oz. Disaronno amaretto
3/4 oz. sweet cream
2 oz. pineapple juice

Blend.

ITALIAN DREAM

1 1/2 oz. Carolans Irish cream
1/2 oz. Disaronno amaretto
2 oz. half-and-half
4 oz. ice cubes

Blend.

ITALIAN ICED TEA

1 oz. Martini & Rossi Rosso vermouth
3 oz. ginger ale

Add ingredients to a tall glass with ice. Garnish with an orange slice.

ITALIAN MARTINI

1 1/2 oz. Vox vodka or Bombay Sapphire gin
dash Disaronno amaretto

Stir with ice. Serve on ice or strain.

ITALIAN MANHATTAN

1/2 oz. Disaronno amaretto
1/4 oz. maraschino cherry juice
1 1/2 oz. Knob Creek bourbon

In a cocktail glass, chilled or rocks glass, add ice, stir, and garnish with an orange slice and a cherry.

ITALIAN WHITE SANGRIA

1 750 ml bottle Martini & Rossi extra dry vermouth
1 cup Cointreau
1 cup juice of three oranges
1/2 cup juice of two lemons
1/4 cup juice of one lime
1/2 cup sugar
1 orange, halved and thinly sliced
1 lemon, halved and thinly sliced
1 apple, cored and thinly sliced
1 cup chilled sparkling water

Combine Martini & Rossi extra dry vermouth, Cointreau, fruit juices, and sugar in a large pitcher. Stir until the sugar is dissolved. Chill until ready to serve. Stir in sliced fruit and sparkling water; serve over ice. Makes seven cups.

J.J.'S SHAMROCK

1 oz. Tullamore Dew Irish whiskey
1/2 oz. DeKuyper white crème de cacao
1/2 oz. DeKuyper green crème de menthe
1 oz. milk

Mix in a shaker or blender with cracked ice and serve in a chilled glass.

JACK ROSE

1 1/2 oz. Laird's applejack
3/4 oz. sweet & sour mix
1 tsp. Rose's grenadine

Shake with ice. Strain.

JACK ROSE COCKTAIL

2 oz. Laird's applejack
1 oz. lemon juice
1/2 oz. grenadine

Shake well with ice and strain into a cocktail glass or serve over ice.

JADE

1 1/2 oz. Bacardi light rum
3/4 oz. lime juice
1 barspoon sugar
dash Cointreau
dash DeKuyper green crème de menthe

Shake with ice and serve over ice.

JAMAICAN DUST

1 part Bacardi rum
1 part Tia Maria
1 part pineapple juice

Shake with ice and strain into a shot glass.

JAMIE'S HIGHLAND SPECIAL

1 part DeKuyper green crème de menthe
1 part Galliano
1 part DeKuyper blackberry liqueur
1 part Kirschwasser

Layer this drink in the order listed. Start with crème de menthe on the bottom and finish Kirschwasser on top.

JAPANESE SLIPPER

1 oz. Cointreau
1/2 oz. DeKuyper melon liqueur
1/2 oz. lemon

Shake. Serve straight on the rocks or straight up.

JASMINE

1/2 oz. Cointreau
1 oz. Bombay Sapphire gin
1/2 oz. Campari
2 oz. lemon juice

Shake with ice. Serve straight up or on the rocks.

JELLY BEAN

1 part DeKuyper anisette
1 part DeKuyper blackberry brandy

You can strain this one into a shot glass or serve on the rocks.

JELLY BEAN II

1 part DeKuyper peppermint schnapps
1 part DeKuyper blackberry brandy

You can strain or serve this on the rocks.

JELLYFISH

1 part Carolans Irish cream
1 part DeKuyper white crème de cacao
1 part Disaronno amaretto
1 part Rose's grenadine

Pour first three ingredients directly into the glass. Pour Rose's grenadine in the center of the glass.

JERSEY BOUNCE

1 1/2 oz. Laird's applejack
dash Cointreau
dash Rose's lime juice
1 1/2 oz. sweet & sour mix
1 1/2 oz. cranberry juice
dash egg white, if desired

Shake well and garnish with wedge of lime.

JERSEY DEVIL

1 1/2 oz. Laird's applejack
1/2 oz. Cointreau
1/2 tsp. sugar
1/2 oz. Rose's lime juice
1/2 oz. cranberry juice

Shake well with ice and strain into a cocktail glass.

JOCOSE JULEP

1/2 oz. Knob Creek bourbon
1/2 oz. DeKuyper green crème de menthe
1 oz. lime juice
1 tsp. sugar
5 chopped mint leaves
club soda

*Combine all ingredients except club soda in blender with-
out ice. Pour into a collins glass over ice cubes. Fill with
club soda and decorate with a sprig of mint.*

JOHN COLLINS

1 oz. Knob Creek bourbon
1/2 oz. sugar syrup
juice of 1/2 lime
club soda

*Pour lemon juice, syrup, and bourbon in a highball glass
filled with ice. Squeeze in the juice from 1/2 lime and
save the shell. Fill the glass with club soda. Stir.*

JOLLEE-RANCHER

1 oz. DeKuyper Peachtree schnapps
1/2 oz. DeKuyper Pucker sour apple
1/2 oz. cranberry juice

Shake and serve over rocks.

JOLLY ROGER

1/2 oz. Drambuie
1 1/2 oz. Bacardi light rum
1 oz. fresh lime juice
1/4 tsp. Dewar's scotch
sparkling water

Combine all ingredients, except sparkling water, with cracked ice in a cocktail shaker. Shake well and pour into a chilled highball glass. Fill with sparkling water and stir gently.

JOURNALIST MARTINI

1 1/2 oz. Bombay Sapphire gin
1/4 oz. Martini & Rossi Rosso vermouth
1/4 oz. Martini & Rossi dry vermouth
dash Angostura bitters
dash lemon juice
dash DeKuyper orange curacao

Stir with ice. Serve over ice or strain.

JUICE FRUIT MARTINI

1/2 oz. Bombay Sapphire gin
1/2 oz. Cointreau
squeezed lemon
splash orange juice

Serve chilled and straight up with a lemon twist.

The Parish Cafe
Boston, MA

JUICY FRUIT

1 part Vox vodka
1 part DeKuyper Peachtree schnapps
1 part DeKuyper melon liqueur
1 part pineapple juice

Shake with ice and strain into a shot glass.

KAMIKAZE

1 oz. Vox vodka
1/2 oz. Cointreau
1/4 oz. Rose's lime juice

Shake with ice and strain into a shot glass.

KENTUCKY BLIZZARD

1 1/2 oz. Knob Creek bourbon
2 oz. cranberry juice
1/2 oz. lime juice
1 tsp. sugar

Shake all ingredients with cracked ice. Strain into cocktail glass or over fresh cracked ice in old-fashioned glass. Garnish with a half-slice of orange.

KENTUCKY COCKTAIL

1 1/2 oz. Knob Creek bourbon
1 oz. pineapple juice

Shake with ice and strain into a cocktail glass.

KENTUCKY COLONEL COCKTAIL

1 1/2 oz. Knob Creek bourbon
1/2 oz. Benedictine

Stir with ice; strain into a cocktail glass. Add a twist of lemon.

KEY LIME HIGH

1/2 oz. Cointreau
1/2 oz. Liquore Galliano
1/2 oz. orange juice
splash lime
splash half-and-half

Shake with ice and strain. Makes two.

KEY WEST MARTINI

1 oz. Vox vodka
1/2 oz. Bacardi Cóco
1/2 oz. DeKuyper melon liqueur
1/2 oz. DeKuyper Peachtree schnapps
1/2 oz. cranberry juice

Shake with ice and strain into a martini glass.

KILLER KOOL-AID

1 part Chambord
1 part Vox vodka
1 part Bombay Sapphire gin
1 part Bacardi light rum
2 oz. cranberry juice
1 oz. sweet & sour mix

Combine in a tall glass over ice.

KILTED BLACK LEPRECHAUN

1/2 oz. Drambuie
1 oz. Carolans Irish cream
1/2 oz. Bacardi light rum

Shake with ice. Strain. Serve as a shot.

KILTLIFTER

1 oz. Drambuie
1 oz. Dewar's scotch
splash Rose's lime juice

Shake with ice. Serve over rocks.

KING ALPHONSE

1 part DeKuyper dark crème de cacao
1 part cream

Layer the cream on top of the DeKuyper dark crème de cacao.

KIR OR KIR ROYALE

3 oz. champagne
splash DeKuyper crème de cassis

Fill the glass with champagne and add a splash of crème de cassis.

KNOB CREEK BOURBON SLING

2 oz. Knob Creek bourbon
1 tsp. superfine sugar
2 tsp. water
1 oz. lemon juice

Shake well. Strain into a glass. Top with a lemon twist.

KNOB CREEK BOURBON STREET

1 1/2 oz. Knob Creek bourbon
1/2 oz. Disaronno amaretto

Shake with ice and strain into a shot glass.

KNUCKLE-BUSTER
(AKA KNUCKLEDUSTER)

1/2 oz. Drambuie
1 1/2 oz. Dewar's scotch
1 tsp. Bacardi 151 rum

In an old-fashioned glass, pour over ice. Stir.

LA BOMBA

1 1/4 oz. Jose Cuervo 1800 tequila
3/4 oz. Cointreau
1 1/2 oz. pineapple juice
1 1/2 oz. orange juice
2 dashes Rose's grenadine

Pour into glass and add Rose's grenadine. Garnish with a lime wheel.

LA JOLLARITA

1 1/2 oz. Jose Cuervo Traditional tequila
1/2 oz. Cointreau
1/2 oz. Chambord

Shake, strain, and serve.

LADIES' CHOICE MARTINI

1 1/2 oz. Vox vodka
dash Martini & Rossi extra dry vermouth
1/4 oz. kummel

Stir with ice and strain.

LADY SCARLETT

1/2 oz. Cointreau
1 oz. Bombay Sapphire gin
1/4 oz. Martini & Rossi dry vermouth
1/4 oz. lime juice
dash bitters

Shake with ice. Serve over ice.

LASER DISK

1/2 oz. Drambuie
1/2 oz. Dewar's scotch
1/2 oz. lemonade

Shake. Serve in a shot glass.

LEAP FROG

1 oz. Bacardi O
1 oz. Cointreau
1 1/2 oz. sweet & sour mix
1/2 oz. fresh-squeezed
orange juice

Shake; garnish with a lime and two maraschino cherries on each end of the lime (the frog).

LEMON CHIFFON

1/2 oz. Cointreau
1 oz. Vox vodka
1 oz. sweet & sour mix

Shake ingredients with ice and serve over ice. Squeeze and drop in a fresh lemon wedge.

LEMON ICE

1 1/4 oz. Vox vodka
1/2 oz. Cointreau
1 1/2 oz. sweet & sour mix
1/2 oz. lemon juice

Build over ice and fill with lemon-lime soda in a 10 oz. glass. Garnish with a lemon slice.

LEPRECHAUN

2 oz. Tullamore Dew Irish whiskey
3 oz. tonic water
3–4 ice cubes
twist lemon peel

Stir gently. Drop in a lemon peel.

LICORICE STICK

1 part Cointreau
1 part Vox vodka
1 part DeKuyper anisette

Shake with ice and strain into a shot glass.

LIFESAVER

1 part Bacardi rum
1 part Vox vodka
1 part DeKuyper melon liqueur
1 part lemon-lime soda

Shake with ice and strain into a shot glass.

LIME ISLAND ICED TEA

3 oz. Vox vodka
1 1/2 oz. Cointreau
4 oz. iced tea
2 tbsp. Rose's lime juice

*Combine iced tea, Vox vodka, Cointreau, and lime juice,
shake and strain into a collins glass filled with ice.*

LIMESTONE

2 oz. Knob Creek bourbon
1 1/2 oz. Collins mix/lemon juice
splash lime juice

Into an ice-filled highball glass, pour bourbon and fill glass with Collins mix; add lime juice.

LIMÓN & CRANBERRY

1 part Bacardi Limón
4 parts cranberry juice

Pour ingredients over ice in a rocks glass. Garnish with a lemon twist.

LIMÓN BAYBREEZE

1 1/2 oz. Bacardi Limón
2 oz. cranberry juice
2 oz. pineapple juice

Pour Limón into a tall glass with ice. Fill with equal parts cranberry and pineapple juice. Garnish with a pineapple wedge.

LIMÓN COSMO

2 oz. Bacardi Limón
1/2 oz. Cointreau
1/2 oz. lime juice
2 oz. cranberry juice

Shake with ice; strain into a chilled martini glass.

LIMÓN SEABREEZE

1 1/2 oz. Bacardi Limón
2 oz. cranberry juice
2 oz. grapefruit juice

Pour Limón into tall glass with ice. Fill with equal parts cranberry and grapefruit juice.

LIPSMACKER

2 oz. DeKuyper Pucker Cheri-Beri
1/2 oz. Rose's lime juice
splash club soda

Serve over ice.

LITTLE DEVIL

drop Tabasco sauce
lemon slice
drop Worcestershire sauce
1/2 oz. lime or lemon juice
1/2 oz. Cointreau
1 oz. Bombay Sapphire gin
tomato juice

Pour all ingredients (except tomato juice) into a tumbler glass with ice. Fill with tomato juice. Stir.

LIZARD SLIME

1 1/2 oz. Jose Cuervo Mistico tequila
1/2 oz. DeKuyper melon liqueur

In a shot glass, float the DeKuyper on top of the Cuervo.

LOCH LOMOND

1/2 oz. Drambuie
1 oz. Dewar's scotch
1/2 oz. Martini & Rossi dry vermouth
1 lemon twist

In a mixing glass half filled with ice, combine the Dewar's, Drambuie, and Martini & Rossi vermouth. Stir well. Strain into a cocktail glass. Garnish with the lemon twist.

LONG ISLAND ICED TEA

1/2 oz. Vox vodka
1/2 oz. Bacardi rum
1/2 oz. Bombay dry gin
1/2 oz. Cointreau
1/2 oz. Jose Cuervo tequila
cola

Shake the first five ingredients over ice and strain into a glass. Fill with cola.

LOUISVILLE COOLER

1 1/2 oz. Knob Creek bourbon
2 oz. orange juice
1 tbs. lime juice
1 tsp. powdered sugar

Shake all ingredients with cracked ice. Strain into an old-fashioned glass over crushed ice. Garnish with an orange wheel.

LOUISVILLE LADY

1 1/4 oz. Knob Creek bourbon
3/4 oz. DeKuyper white crème de cacao
1 oz. cream

Shake and strain into a cocktail glass.

LOVER'S KISS

1 oz. Disaronno amaretto
1/2 oz. DeKuyper cherry brandy
1/2 oz. DeKuyper dark crème de cacao
1 oz. cream or half-and-half

Shake with ice. Strain into a chilled martini glass. Garnish with a maraschino cherry.

LUCK OF THE IRISH

2 oz. Carolans Irish cream liqueur
2 oz. Tullamore Dew Irish whiskey
1 oz. Irish Mist

Shake.

LUCKY BOY

1/2 oz. lime juice
2 oz. grapefruit juice
1 1/2 oz. Cointreau
soda water
mint cordial

Shake lime juice, grapefruit juice, and Cointreau with ice. Strain into a tumbler glass with ice. Fill with soda water. Add a drop of mint cordial. Stir. Garnish with a lime slice and a maraschino cherry.

LUCKY LADY

3/4 oz. Bacardi light rum
1/4 oz. DeKuyper anisette
1/4 oz. DeKuyper white crème de cacao
3/4 oz. cream

Blend with crushed ice and serve in a margarita glass.

MACARENA

1 oz. Jose Cuervo Especial tequila
1/2 oz. Bacardi Cóco
3 oz. sweet & sour mix
1 oz. orange juice
1 oz. pineapple juice
splash cranberry juice

Shake and pour over ice into a tall glass. Garnish with pineapple, orange, and a maraschino cherry.

MAD MARTINI

1 part DeKuyper Mad Melon liqueur
2 parts Vox vodka
splash lime juice

Garnish with a lemon twist.

MAD PUCKER

2/3 oz. DeKuyper Mad Melon liqueur
1/3 oz. DeKuyper Pucker sour apple

Shake. Strain into a shot glass.

MADRAS

1 1/4 oz. Vox vodka
2 oz. cranberry juice
2 oz. orange juice

Pour Vox vodka over ice in a tall glass. Fill half way with orange juice and top it off with cranberry juice.

MAGNOLIA MAIDEN

1 1/4 oz. Knob Creek bourbon
1 1/4 oz. Cointreau
splash simple syrup
splash club soda

Shake bourbon, Cointreau, and simple syrup. Strain into a glass with ice. Top with club soda.

MAI TAI

3/4 oz. Bacardi light rum
1/4 oz. Bacardi 151 rum
1/2 oz. DeKuyper orange curacao
1/2 oz. Rose's lime juice
1/4 oz. orgeat syrup
1/4 oz. simple syrup

Stir with ice. Garnish with mint, maraschino cherry, and pineapple.

MAIDEN'S PRAYER

2 parts Bombay dry gin
2 parts Cointreau
1 part orange juice
1 part lemon juice

Shake with ice and strain into a glass.

MAIDEN'S PRAYER II

1/2 oz. Cointreau
1 oz. Bombay Sapphire gin
1/2 oz. Bacardi light rum
2 oz. lemon juice

Shake with ice. Serve over ice or straight up.

MAIN SQUEEZE

1 1/2 oz. DeKuyper Wild Strawberry liqueur
2 oz. cranberry juice
2 oz. orange juice
club soda

Combine first three ingredients in a tall glass and top with club soda.

MANGO FROZEN MARGARITA

1 1/2 parts Jose Cuervo Especial
3 parts Jose Cuervo margarita mix
1 cup diced, peeled ripe mango
1 1/2 tbs. superfine granulated sugar
1 cup ice cubes

Blend all ingredients in a blender until smooth. Pour into a margarita glass.

MANHATTAN

2 oz. Knob Creek bourbon
splash Martini & Rossi Rosso or dry vermouth
dash Angostura bitters

Stir. Garnish with a maraschino cherry.

MARASCHINO

1 1/2 oz. Bombay Sapphire gin
1/2 oz. maraschino cherry juice

Shake. Strain drink into a cocktail glass.

MARGARITA

1 part Jose Cuervo Especial
2 parts sweet & sour mix
1 part lime juice
splash Cointreau

Add salt on the rim of the glass. Shake and serve on the rocks.

MARGARITA MADRES

1 1/4 oz. Jose Cuervo gold tequila
1/2 oz. Cointreau
1 1/2 oz. sweet & sour mix
1 1/2 oz. orange juice
1 1/2 oz. cranberry juice

Blend with crushed ice. Serve in a tall glass. Garnish with a lime.

MARGARITA PERFECT CUERVO

1 1/2 parts Jose Cuervo Especial
3 parts Jose Cuervo margarita mix
1/2 cup crushed ice
salt
lime wedge

Mix all ingredients (except salt and lime) in a blender. Rub the rim of a margarita glass with lime and then dip into salt to frost. Pour into a glass and garnish with a lime wedge.

MARGARITA SPRITZER

1 1/2 parts Jose Cuervo Especial
3 parts Jose Cuervo margarita mix
chilled seltzer or club soda
1 lime slice

In a margarita glass, combine Jose Cuervo Especial, Jose Cuervo margarita mix, and four ice cubes. Fill the glass with the seltzer and stir the drink. Garnish with the lime slice.

MARTINI

2 oz. Bombay Sapphire gin
dash Martini & Rossi extra dry vermouth

Shake or stir Bombay Sapphire gin and vermouth over ice. Strain and serve in a cocktail glass straight up or over ice. Garnish with a twist or an olive.

MARTINI BELLINI

2 oz. Vox vodka or Bombay Sapphire gin
1/4 oz. DeKuyper Peachtree schnapps

Shake or stir Vox vodka or Bombay Sapphire gin and DeKuyper Peachtree schnapps over ice. Strain and serve.

MARY PICKFORD

1 1/2 oz. Bacardi light rum
1 1/2 oz. pineapple juice
splash Rose's grenadine

Shake with crushed ice. Serve over ice or strain.

MELON BALL

3/4 oz. DeKuyper melon liqueur
1 oz. Vox vodka
4 oz. orange juice

Combine in a glass and stir.

MELON CITRUS COOLER

1 part DeKuyper Pucker watermelon schnapps
1 part Vox vodka

Fill with orange juice and serve over ice.

MELONTINI

1 part DeKuyper Pucker watermelon schnapps
1 part Vox vodka
splash lemon-lime soda

Garnish with a watermelon slice.

MELORITA

1 part DeKuyper Pucker watermelon schnapps
1 part Jose Cuervo tequila
2 parts sweet & sour mix

Salt rim of glass and serve over crushed ice.

METROPOLITAN

1 oz. Martini & Rossi Rosso vermouth
2 oz. Hennessy cognac
1/2 tsp. sugar syrup
2 dashes Angostura bitters
4-5 ice cubes

Shake and strain into a chilled martini glass.

MEXI-COLA

1 part Jose Cuervo Clásico
4 parts cola soda

*Combine Cuervo and soda in a rocks glass with ice.
Garnish with a lime wedge.*

MEXICAN BANANA

1 1/2 oz. Jose Cuervo tequila
3/4 oz. DeKuyper crème de banana

Pour ingredients into a rocks glass filled with ice.

MEXICAN BERRY

1 oz. Chambord
1 oz. Jose Cuervo tequila

Shake with ice and strain into a shot glass.

MEXICAN PAINKILLER

1/2 oz. Jose Cuervo tequila
1/2 oz. Vox vodka
1/2 oz. Bacardi light rum
1 oz. pineapple juice
1/2 oz. orange juice
2 tbs. Coco Lopez cream of coconut

Combine, blend, and pour.

MEXICAROLANS

1 part Carolans Irish cream
1 part Jose Cuervo tequila

Shake and serve over ice.

MEXICO MARTINI

1 1/2 oz. Jose Cuervo tequila
1 tbs. Martini & Rossi extra dry vermouth
2-3 drops vanilla extract

Shake and strain into an iced glass.

MEXICO ROSE

1/2 oz. Jose Cuervo tequila
1 oz. lime juice
1/2 oz. Rose's grenadine (or DeKuyper crème de
    cassis)

Combine in a rocks glass filled with ice.

MIAMI SPECIAL

1 oz. Bacardi light rum
1/4 oz. DeKuyper white crème de menthe
3/4 oz. lemon or Rose's lime juice

Blend.

MIDNIGHT MARTINI

1 1/2 oz. Vox vodka
1/2 oz. Chambord

Stir with ice and strain. Garnish with a lemon twist.

Gallery Lounge Sheraton
Seattle, WA

MILK & HONEY

Equal parts:
    Irish Mist
    Carolans Irish cream

Served in a rocks glass.

MIMOSA

3 oz. champagne
2 oz. orange juice

Combine in a champagne flute and stir.

MINT COOLER

1 oz. Bombay Sapphire gin
1/4 oz. DeKuyper peppermint schnapps
club soda

In a tall glass with ice, combine the first two ingredients.
Fill the glass with club soda.

MINT JULEP

8 mint sprigs
1 tsp. superfine sugar
2 tsp. water
2 1/2 oz. Knob Creek bourbon

In silver mug, muddle mint leaves, superfine sugar, and water. Fill glass or mug with crushed ice and add Knob Creek. Garnish with a mint sprig.

MINTA

2 oz. Vox vodka
fresh crushed mint
1 tsp. sugar

Shake and serve over crushed ice.

MINTINI OR BOMBAY SAPPHIRE GIN STINGER

2 parts Bombay Sapphire gin
1 part DeKuyper white crème de menthe

Stir gently with ice and strain.

MIST OLD FASHIONED

1 1/4 oz. Irish Mist
orange slice
cherry bitters
sugar
club soda or water

Muddle the orange, cherry bitters, and sugar. Add Irish Mist. Top with club soda or water.

MISTER MURPHY

1 part Irish Mist
1 part Bacardi rum
1 part orange juice

Serve in a rocks glass with a dash of Angostura bitters.

MISTER MURPHY II

1 part Irish Mist
1 part Bacardi rum
1 part orange juice
dash Angostura bitters

Combine in a rocks glass over ice with a dash of Angostura bitters.

MISTIC BEACH

1 1/4 oz. Jose Cuervo Mistico tequila
3/4 oz. Cointreau
3 oz. cranberry juice

Combine over ice in a tall glass. Stir. Garnish with a lemon wedge.

MISTIC CHOCKLIC

3/4 oz. Jose Cuervo Mistico tequila
3/4 oz. DeKuyper coffee liqueur
1 oz. orange juice

Shake and strain into a rocks glass with ice.

MISTIC MERLIN

3/4 oz. Jose Cuervo Mistico tequila
3/4 oz. Cointreau
1/2 oz. lime juice

Shake with ice and strain.

MISTIC SHANDY

1 1/4 oz. Jose Cuervo Mistico tequila
7 oz. draft beer

Combine tequila and beer in a glass.

MISTICAL MAYAN

1 1/4 oz. Jose Cuervo Mistico tequila
3 oz. orange juice
lemon-lime soda

Stir the first two ingredients with ice in a tall glass. Fill with lemon-lime soda. Garnish with a lime wedge.

MISTICO BANDITO

1 oz. Jose Cuervo Mistico tequila
1 oz. cranberry juice
1 oz. black cherry juice

Shake and serve in a shot glass.

MISTICO BERRY

1 oz. Jose Cuervo Mistico tequila
1 oz. cabernet wine
splash Cointreau
splash lime juice
splash lemon-lime soda
sweet & sour mix

Combine first five ingredients in a tall glass with ice. Fill with sweet & sour mix and garnish with a lemon wedge.

MISTICO CALIENTE

2 oz. Jose Cuervo Mistico tequila
splash Tabasco sauce

Combine in a shot glass and drop into a draft beer.

MISTICO CARIBBEAN SEA

1 1/4 oz. Jose Cuervo Mistico tequila
3/4 oz. DeKuyper blue curacao
1/2 oz. DeKuyper Peachtree schnapps
sweet & sour mix

*Combine first three ingredients in a tall glass over ice.
Fill with sweet & sour mix.*

MISTICO DESERT BERRY

1 1/2 oz. Jose Cuervo Mistico tequila
dash Chambord

Stir and strain into a shot glass.

MISTICO LEMONADE

1 oz. Jose Cuervo Mistico tequila
1 oz. DeKuyper orange curacao
1 oz. club soda
1 oz. cranberry juice
juice from 1/2 lemon

Serve in a tall glass over ice.

MISTICO MARTINI

1 oz. Jose Cuervo Mistico tequila
1 oz. Chambord
1 oz. sweet & sour mix

Stir with ice and strain into a martini glass.

MISTICO MIRAGE

1 1/2 oz. Jose Cuervo Mistico tequila
1 1/2 oz. orange juice
1 1/2 oz. tonic water

Stir with ice and garnish with a lime wedge.

MISTICO MISSILE

1 oz. Jose Cuervo Mistico tequila
1/2 oz. DeKuyper Peachtree schnapps
splash grapefruit juice

Shake and strain. Serve in a shot glass.

MISTIC MORNING

1 oz. Jose Cuervo Mistico tequila
1 oz. pineapple juice
1 oz. orange juice
splash Cointreau
Rose's grenadine

Combine first four ingredients. Float grenadine on top. Garnish with lime.

MISTICO MYSTERY

1 oz. Jose Cuervo Mistico tequila
1 oz. Cointreau
1 oz. pineapple juice

Shake and strain into a shot glass.

MISTICO SLIDE

1/2 oz. DeKuyper coffee liqueur
1/2 oz. Carolans Irish cream
1/2 oz. Jose Cuervo Mistico tequila

Layer ingredients in order listed, starting with DeKuyper coffee liqueur in a shot glass.

MISTICO SPIKE

1 1/2 oz. Jose Cuervo Mistico tequila
3 oz. grapefruit juice
dash bitters

Stir with ice. Garnish with an orange wedge.

MISTICO VERTIGO

1 1/4 oz. Jose Cuervo Mistico tequila
2 oz. sweet & sour mix
1 oz. cranberry juice
juice from 1/2 lemon

Stir with ice. Garnish with an orange wheel.

MISTRAL

1 oz. Chambord
2 oz. dry white wine
1 tbs. frozen strawberries or raspberries

Mix in a blender with ice and pour into a champagne glass.

MISTY MIST

1 1/4 oz. Irish Mist

Serve on shaved ice.

MOCHA MELT

1 oz. Jose Cuervo gold tequila
5 oz. freshly brewed, strong, hot coffee
1 pkg. hot cocoa mix (single-serving packet)
1/2 oz. DeKuyper coffee liqueur
whipped cream

Combine ingredients in a glass and stir. Top with whipped cream.

MOCHA BERRY

2 oz. Chambord
1/2 oz. DeKuyper dark crème de cacao
hot coffee
whipped cream

Serve in a coffee cup or mug.

MOCHA MINT

3/4 oz. coffee brandy
3/4 oz. DeKuyper white crème de menthe
3/4 oz. DeKuyper white crème de cacao

Combine ingredients in a glass and stir. Strain into a cocktail glass.

MOCKINGBIRD

1 1/4 oz. Jose Cuervo tequila
2 tsp. DeKuyper white crème de menthe
1 oz. fresh lime juice

Shake and strain into a chilled cocktail glass with ice.

MODERN LOVE

1/2 oz. orange juice
1 1/2 oz. grapefruit juice
1 oz. Bombay Sapphire gin
1 1/2 oz. Cointreau
grapefruit peel spiral

Shake all ingredients with ice. Strain into a tumbler glass, over crushed ice. Stir.

MOJITO

2 oz. Bacardi light rum
8 mint leaves
juice of 1/2 lime
2 tsp. sugar
club soda

In a collins glass place mint leaves and lime, crush with a muddler or the back of a spoon, add sugar. Fill glass with ice, add Bacardi, and top with club soda. Stir well and garnish with a sprig of mint.

MONKEY GLAND

2 oz. Bombay Sapphire gin
3 oz. orange juice
1/4 oz. absinthe/anis
shot Rose's grenadine

Serve in a tall glass.

MOONLIGHT MARGARITA

1 1/2 oz. Jose Cuervo gold tequila
1 oz. DeKuyper blue curacao
1 oz. lime juice

Rub the rim of a margarita glass with lime rind and dip it into salt. Blend ingredients and serve in the prepared salt glass. Garnish with a lime slice.

MOONRAKER

2 parts Jose Cuervo Especial
4 parts pineapple juice
1 1/2 parts DeKuyper blue curacao

Pour the Jose Cuervo Especial and pineapple juice into a rocks glass almost filled with ice cubes. Stir well. Drop the curacao into the center of the drink.

MOONSHOT

1 1/4 oz. Bombay Sapphire gin
3 oz. clam juice
dash red pepper sauce

Stir over ice cubes.

MORNING GLORY

1/4 pink grapefruit, chopped
1 passion fruit
2 tsp. fine sugar
3/4 oz. Chambord
ice
champagne

Shake all but champagne. Top with champagne.

MOTHER PUCKER

1 oz. DeKuyper Pucker sour apple
1 oz. DeKuyper Pucker Cheri-Beri
1 oz. DeKuyper Pucker grape schnapps
splash orange juice
squeeze lime
1 maraschino cherry

Shake and serve in a tall glass with ice.

MOUNT GRINDER

1 1/2 oz. Bacardi rum
2 oz. cranberry juice
splash lemon-lime soda

Combine in a tall glass.

MOUNTAIN MELTER

1 oz. Jose Cuervo gold tequila
1/2 oz. Cointreau
5 oz. hot water
hot cocoa mix (1 single-serving packet)

Combine ingredients in a glass and stir. Top with whipped cream and ground cinnamon.

MS. TEA

1 1/4 oz. Irish Mist
3 oz. iced tea

Mix with ice; serve over ice.

MUDSLIDE

1/4 oz. DeKuyper coffee liqueur
1 oz. Vox vodka
1/4 oz. Carolans Irish cream
cola

Combine first three ingredients in a glass with ice and fill with cola.

MUDSLIDE II

3/4 oz. DeKuyper coffee liqueur
3/4 oz. Carolans Irish cream

Pour over ice in a rocks glass.

MURPH'S DREAM

1 part Irish Mist
1 part Vox vodka
1 part lemon juice
sugar

Shake. Serve straight up or over ice.

MURPHY'S DREAM

1 part Irish Mist
1 part Bombay Sapphire gin
1 part lemon juice
sugar

Shake. Serve straight up or on the rocks.

NAKED MARTINI

2 oz. Vox vodka or Bombay Sapphire gin

Serve over ice.

NARRAGANSETT

1 1/2 oz. Knob Creek bourbon
1/2 oz. Martini & Rossi Rosso vermouth
3 dashes DeKuyper anisette

Stir in old-fashioned glass with ice cubes. Add a twist of lemon peel.

NATION COCKTAIL

1 1/2 oz. Jose Cuervo gold tequila
1 1/2 oz. pineapple juice
1 1/2 oz. orange juice
1/4 oz. DeKuyper blue curacao

Combine the first three ingredients over ice. Float blue curacao. You can also serve this one without ice.

NEGRONI

1 part Campari
1 part Vox vodka
1 part Martini & Rossi Rosso vermouth

Shake and serve on the rocks or straight up.

NELLIE JANE

1 1/4 oz. Irish Mist
1/4 oz. DeKuyper Peachtree schnapps
3 oz. orange juice
1 oz. ginger ale

Mix all but ginger ale. Float ginger ale.

NERVOUS BREAKDOWN

1 1/2 oz. Vox vodka
1/2 oz. Chambord
splash cranberry juice
soda

Combine the first three ingredients in a tall glass. Fill with soda.

NEW YORKER

1 oz. Knob Creek bourbon
2 oz. cranberry juice
2 oz. grapefruit juice
1/2 oz. Rose's lime juice
1/4 oz. Rose's grenadine

Stir ingredients together and serve over ice in a wine glass.

NEWTON'S COCKTAIL

1 1/4 oz. DeKuyper Pucker sour apple
3/4 oz. DeKuyper melon liqueur
3 oz. sweet & sour mix

NIGHT AND DAY

1/2 part Jose Cuervo Especial
1/2 part DeKuyper coffee liqueur
1/2 part cola

Pour all the ingredients into a shot glass.

NUT 'N' HOLLI

1 part Irish Mist
1 part Disaronno amaretto
1 part Carolans Irish cream

Shake. Serve straight up in a shot glass.

NUTS & BERRIES

1/2 oz. Vox vodka
1/2 oz. Disaronno amaretto
1/2 oz. DeKuyper coffee liqueur
1/4 oz. cream

Combine with ice and shake. Strain and serve straight up in a rocks glass.

NUTS AND CHERRYS

1 oz. DeKuyper Cheri-Beri Pucker
1/2 oz. Disaronno amaretto

Shake with ice, strain into a shot glass.

N.Y. COSMO

1 1/2 oz. Vox vodka
1/2 oz. Chambord
1 oz. sweet & sour mix
2 oz. cranberry juice
dash orange juice
ice

Shake and pour over ice in a cocktail glass.

O & CRANBERRY

1 1/2 oz. Bacardi O
5 oz. cranberry juice
orange wedge
garnish

Stir in a tall glass over ice.

O & CREAM

1 1/2 oz. Bacardi O
1 1/2 oz. Carolans Irish cream

Shake with ice. Serve in a shooter glass or a rocks glass over ice.

O & TONIC

1 1/2 oz. Bacardi O
6 oz. tonic water
orange twist
garnish

Serve in a tall glass with ice.

O BIG DADDY (FROM TU TU TANGO)

1/2 oz. Bacardi O
1/2 oz. Bacardi Razz
1/4 oz. pineapple juice
1/4 oz. cranberry juice

Combine all into shaker, strain into martini glass, sink grenadine garnish with orange twist.

O CIRCLE MARTINI

1 1/2 oz. Bacardi O
1/2 oz. Bombay Sapphire gin
splash cream

*Shake with ice; strain and serve in chilled martini glass;
garnish with an orange twist.*

O COSMOPOLITAN

2 oz. Bacardi O
1 oz. Cointreau
1/2 oz. lime juice
splash cranberry juice
orange wedge
garnish

Serve on the rocks with an orange wedge.

O LOOK MARTINI COCKTAIL

2 oz. Bacardi O
1/2 oz. pink grapefruit juice
1/2 oz. Cointreau
1/2 oz. sweet & sour mix
splash lemon-lime soda

Serve up in a sugar-rimmed glass; garnish with a grapefruit slice.

O MADRAS

1 1/2 oz. Bacardi O
4 oz. cranberry juice
1 oz. orange juice

Blend with ice; serve in a tall glass garnished with a maraschino cherry and an orange slice.

O MY MARTINI COCKTAIL

2 oz. Bacardi O
1 oz. DeKuyper blue curacao
splash sweet & sour mix

Shake with ice; strain into a chilled martini glass. Top with grenadine.

O.J. MIST

2 oz. Irish Mist
3 oz. orange juice

Combine in a tall glass over ice.

OATMEAL COOKIE

Equal parts:
    Carolans Irish cream
    Goldschlager
    butterscotch schnapps

Shake and serve as a shot.

O-CHERI BABY

1 1/4 oz. DeKuyper Pucker Cheri-Beri, chilled
1/4 oz. Vox vodka

Serve as a shot.

OLD FASHIONED

1 1/2 oz. American or Canadian whisky
1/4 tsp. superfine sugar
2 dashes Angostura bitters
splash of club soda
cherry and orange slice

Muddle the cherry (without stem), orange slice, sugar, and a splash of club soda. Add the remaining ingredients and stir.

OLD LAY

3/4 oz. Cointreau
1 1/4 oz. Jose Cuervo tequila
dash Rose's grenadine
3/4 oz. lime juice

Shake with ice and strain.

OLYMPIC

1 oz. Hennessy cognac
1 oz. Cointreau
1 oz. orange juice

Shake and pour into a chilled cocktail glass.

OOH LA LA MARTINI COCKTAIL

1 oz. Bacardi O
1 oz. orange juice
splash Cointreau

Shake with ice; strain and serve in a chilled martini glass garnished with an orange slice.

ORANGE BLOSSOM

1 1/4 oz. Vox vodka
3 oz. orange juice
1 tsp. superfine sugar

Stir with ice in a tall glass.

ORANGE BLOSSOM II

1 1/4 oz. Vox vodka
1/2 oz. Cointreau
3 oz. orange juice
1 tsp. superfine sugar

Stir with ice in a tall glass.

ORANGE BLOSSOM III

1/4 oz. Bombay Sapphire gin
1 oz. sweetened lemon mix
2 oz. orange juice

Shake with ice and pour on the rocks.

ORANGE CRUSH

1/2 oz. Cointreau
1 oz. Vox vodka
1/2 oz. orange juice
dash lemon-lime soda

Shake with ice and strain. Top with lemon-lime soda.

ORANGE CUERVO RICKEY

2 parts Jose Cuervo Especial
2 tbs. Cointreau
1/2 lime
chilled club soda or seltzer

In a tall highball glass filled with ice cubes, combine Jose Cuervo Especial and Cointreau. Squeeze the lime over the drink and drop the lime into the glass. Top off with club soda.

ORANGE MARGARITA

1 1/2 oz. Jose Cuervo gold tequila
1/2 oz. Cointreau
3 oz. orange juice
1/2 oz. sweet & sour mix

Blend. Garnish with strawberries.

ORANGE RUSH

1 oz. Bacardi O
1/2 oz. DeKuyper Peachtree schnapps
2 oz. orange juice
1 oz. pineapple juice
1 oz. cranberry juice

Blend with ice; serve in a tall glass garnished with an orange slice.

ORANGE SUNSET

1 oz. Bombay Sapphire gin
1/4 oz. DeKuyper crème de banana liqueur
1 oz. sweetened lemon mix
1 oz. orange juice

Shake well with ice and serve on the rocks.

ORANGE WHIP

1 oz. Bacardi O
3/4 oz. Bombay Sapphire gin
2 oz. orange juice
1 oz. sweet & sour mix

Shake with ice; serve in a tall glass with ice and top with grenadine.

ORANGESICLE

1 1/2 oz. Bacardi O
1 1/2 oz. cream
1/2 oz. orange juice

Blend. Serve in a powdered sugar rimmed glass; garnish with an orange wheel.

ORANGETINI

1 1/2 oz. Vox vodka
dash Martini & Rossi extra dry vermouth
splash Cointreau

Stir gently and strain over ice. Garnish with an orange peel.

ORGASM

1 part Carolans Irish cream
1 part Disaronno amaretto
1 part DeKuyper coffee liqueur

Shake with ice and strain into a shot glass.

ORGASM II

1 part Disaronno amaretto
1 part DeKuyper coffee liqueur
1 part Carolans Irish cream
1 part cream

Shake with ice and strain into a shot glass.

ORIENT EXPRESS

1 oz. pineapple juice
1 oz. grapefruit juice
1 oz. Bacardi light rum
1 oz. Cointreau
Rose's grenadine

Shake pineapple juice, grapefruit juice, Bacardi, and Cointreau with ice. Strain into a tumbler glass with ice. Add a drop of grenadine. Stir. Garnish pineapple slice and mint leaves.

OTB

2 oz. Bacardi O
2 oz. iced tea

Serve over crushed ice with splash of soda; garnish with an orange twist.

O MARTINI COCKTAIL

2 oz. Bacardi O
1/4 oz. Martini & Rossi extra dry vermouth
orange twist garnish

Serve in a rocks glass over ice or straight up in a martini glass.

OUTRIGGER

1 oz. Vox vodka
1/2 oz. DeKuyper Peachtree schnapps
dash lime juice
2 oz. pineapple juice

Combine with ice in a shaker and shake. Strain over ice into a rocks glass.

OYSTER SHOOTER

1 oz. Vox vodka
1 raw oyster
1 tsp. cocktail sauce

Pour Vox vodka over the oyster and sauce in a small rocks glass and stir. Add a squeeze of lemon. You can also add a dash of horseradish.

PADDY COCKTAIL

1 1/2 oz. Tullamore Dew Irish whiskey
3/4 oz. Martini & Rossi Rosso vermouth

Several dashes Angostura bitters. Stir.

PADDY O'ROCCO

1 1/2 oz. Irish Mist
3 oz. orange juice
splash Disaronno amaretto

Mix Irish Mist and orange juice. Top with a splash of Disaronno amaretto.

PAISLEY

2 oz. Bombay Sapphire gin
1/2 oz. Dewar's scotch
1/2 oz. Martini & Rossi dry vermouth

Garnish with a twist as you stir.

PALOMA (DOVE)

2 parts Jose Cuervo Especial
lemon-lime soda
lime wedge
salt

Rub the rim of a chilled tall highball glass with lime and dip it into the salt to coat. Put ice into the glass; add Jose Cuervo Especial. Add some more salt if you'd like and fill the glass with the lemon-lime soda. Garnish with lime.

PANZER

1 part Vox vodka
1 part Bombay Sapphire gin
1 part Cointreau

Combine in a shaker with ice. Strain into a chilled cocktail glass.

PEACH BANANA DAIQUIRI

1 1/2 oz. Bacardi light rum
1/2 med. banana, diced
1 oz. fresh lime juice
1/4 cup sliced peaches (fresh, frozen, or canned)

Blend.

PEACH BLOSSOM

1 oz. DeKuyper Peachtree schnapps
1/2 oz. Disaronno amaretto
1 scoop vanilla ice cream

Blend.

PEACH COBBLER

1 1/4 oz. DeKuyper Peachtree schnapps
5 oz. hot apple cider

Serve in a mug. Top with cream.

PEACH CREAMY

3/4 oz. DeKuyper Peachtree schnapps
1/2 oz. DeKuyper white crème de cacao
2 oz. cream

Shake well with ice and strain into a cocktail glass.

PEACH IRISH

1 1/2 oz. Tullamore Dew Irish whiskey
1 ripe peach (peeled, pitted, and sliced)
1/2 cup fresh lime juice
1 oz. DeKuyper apricot brandy
1 tbs. superfine sugar
dash vanilla extract

Blend.

PEACH MARGARITA

1 1/2 oz. Jose Cuervo gold tequila
1 oz. Cointreau
1 oz. lime juice
1/2 cup peaches (canned)

Blend. Garnish with peach slices.

PEACH ON THE BEACH

3/4 oz. DeKuyper Peachtree schnapps
1/2 oz. Vox vodka
2 oz. orange juice
2 oz. cranberry juice

Build over cubed ice in a tall glass.

PHOEBE SNOW

1 1/2 oz. Hennessy cognac
1 1/2 oz. Dubonnet Red
dash Pernod

Shake and pour into a chilled cocktail glass.

PICNIC PUNCH

6 1/2 oz. Jose Cuervo tequila
3 1/2 oz. Chambord
10 oz. fruit puree
3 1/2 oz. mango nectar
7 oz. fruit tea, steeped, sweetened, and chilled
1 lime

Mix in a large punch bowl. Makes 5–6 servings.

PIÑA COLADA

2 oz. Bacardi light rum
6 oz. pineapple juice
2 oz. Coco Lopez cream of coconut

Blend with ice; garnish with a pineapple spear.

PINEAPPLE BOMB

1 part Bacardi light rum
1 part Bacardi dark rum
1 part pineapple juice

Shake with ice and strain into a shot glass.

PINEAPPLE-ORANGE MARGARITA

1 1/2 parts Jose Cuervo Especial
3 parts Jose Cuervo margarita mix
1 part pineapple juice
1 tbs. simple syrup
pineapple spears
maraschino cherries

Combine pineapple juice, Jose Cuervo Especial, Jose Cuervo margarita mix, and simple syrup in large mixing glass. Add ice cubes and stir to blend well. Strain the contents into a margarita glass. Garnish with pineapple spears and maraschino cherries.

PINEAPPLE TWIST

1 1/2 oz. Bacardi rum
6 oz. pineapple juice
splash lemon juice

Shake and pour into a tall glass over ice.

PINK BANANA

2 oz. DeKuyper crème de banana
2 oz. pink lemonade

Shake and serve in a tall glass.

PINK CADDY

1 1/2 parts Jose Cuervo tequila
1 1/2 parts cranberry juice
1/2 part freshly squeezed lime juice
3/4 parts Cointreau

Shake first three ingredients with ice and strain into martini glass. Serve Cointreau in a shot glass as an accompaniment to be poured into the cocktail between sips.

PINK CADILLAC WITH
HAWAIIAN PLATES

1 1/4 oz. Jose Cuervo 1800 tequila
2 oz. pineapple juice
2 oz. cranberry juice
1/2 oz. sweet & sour mix

Combine in a rocks glass. Garnish with a lime wedge.

PINK CREAM FIZZ

2 oz. Bombay Sapphire gin
lemon juice
sugar
light cream
Rose's grenadine
club soda

Top with club soda.

PINK ELEPHANT

splash Rose's grenadine
2 oz. Bombay Sapphire gin

Shake and serve over ice.

PINK ELEPHANT EARS

2 oz. Vox vodka
2 oz. pink lemonade
1/2 lime, freshly squeezed

Shake and serve over ice.

PINK FIX

2 oz. Bombay Sapphire gin
2 oz. lemon juice
splash Rose's grenadine

Shake and serve on the rocks or as a shot.

PINK FLAMINGO

1 oz. DeKuyper Wilderberry schnapps
2 oz. cranberry juice
shot sweet & sour mix

Pour together over ice and stir.

PINK GIN & TONIC

2 oz. Bombay Sapphire gin
tonic water
1/2 oz. Campari
lime slice

Serve in a tall glass.

PINK GIN

2 oz. Bombay Sapphire gin
splash Angostura bitters

Serve over ice.

PINK HEART

1/2 oz. DeKuyper crème de cacao
1/2 oz. Chambord
milk or cream
ice

*Serve in a rocks glass filled with ice. Add crème de cacao
and Chambord. Fill with cream or milk. Stir.*

PINK HOUND

1 part Vox vodka
1 part Bombay Sapphire gin
3 parts pink grapefruit juice

Shake ingredients with ice and strain into a glass.

PINK LADY

3 oz. Bombay Sapphire gin
5 dashes Rose's grenadine
2 oz. half-and-half or vanilla ice cream

Shake or blend; garnish with maraschino cherry.

PINK LEMONADE

2 oz. Vox vodka
1 oz. sweet & sour mix
1 oz. cranberry juice
1/2 oz. lime juice

Shake and serve in a tall glass.

PINK LEMONADE II

1 1/4 oz. Vox vodka
1 oz. cranberry juice
1 1/4 oz. sweet & sour mix
1/2 tsp. sugar
club soda

Combine Vox vodka, sugar, sweet & sour mix, and cranberry juice in a tall glass. Stir to dissolve sugar. Add ice and top with club soda. Add a squeeze of lime.

PINK LIMÓN

2 oz. Bacardi Limón
1 oz. sweet & sour mix
2 oz. cranberry juice
1/2 oz. Rose's grenadine
2 oz. cream or half-and-half

Shake or blend.

PINK PANTHER

1 1/2 oz. Jose Cuervo tequila
3/4 oz. lemon juice
3/4 oz. cream
1/2 oz. Rose's grenadine

Blend with crushed ice and strain into a chilled glass.

PINK PANTHER II

1 1/4 oz. Bacardi light rum
3/4 oz. lemon juice
3/4 oz. cream
1/2 oz. Rose's grenadine

Blend with crushed ice and strain.

PINK PANTHER III

2 1/2oz. Bacardi Còco
1 oz. Vox vodka
1/2 oz. DeKuyper Peachtree schnapps
1/2 oz. Cointreau
splash grapefruit
splash orange juice
dash Rose's grenadine

Shake and strain ingredients into a chilled 10 oz. martini glass. Sink a splash of grenadine syrup and garnish with an orange wheel.

PINK PILLOW

2 oz. Vox vodka
splash Rose's grenadine
2 oz. sweet & sour mix

Shake with ice. Serve in a tall glass.

PINK PITCH

2 oz. Vox vodka
1/2 oz. Licor 43
1/2 oz. milk
splash Rose's grenadine

Shake with ice and serve on the rocks.

PINK PONY

2 parts Jose Cuervo Especial
1/3 cup chilled cranberry juice
1/4 cup chilled apple juice
chilled club soda or seltzer water

In a rocks glass filled with ice cubes, combine the Jose Cuervo Especial, the cranberry juice, and the apple juice. Top off the drink with the club soda.

PINK PUSSYCAT

1 1/2 oz. Bombay Sapphire gin
1/4 oz. Chambord
2 1/4 oz. pineapple juice
splash Rose's grenadine

Shake and serve over ice.

PINK PUSSYCAT II

1 1/2 oz. Vox vodka
1/2 oz. pineapple juice
splash Rose's grenadine

Pour over ice into a highball glass. Garnish with a sliced strawberry.

PINK RANGER

1 oz. Vox vodka
1/2 oz. Coco Lopez cream of coconut
1 oz. DeKuyper Peachtree schnapps
1 oz. cranberry juice
1 oz. pineapple juice

Blend and serve in a tall glass.

PINK ROSE

2 oz. Vox vodka
1/2 oz. DeKuyper Peachtree schnapps
dash cranberry juice

Shake and serve on the rocks.

PINK RUSSIAN

1 oz. tequila rose
1/2 oz. DeKuyper coffee liqueur
1/2 oz. Vox vodka
1/2 oz. milk

Shake and serve on the rocks.

PINK SIN MARTINI

3/4 part DeKuyper cinnamon schnapps
1 part DeKuyper white crème de cacao
1 1/2 parts Vox vodka
1 part cranberry juice

Shake and strain into a glass.

PINK SQUIRREL

1 oz. crème de noyaux
1 oz. DeKuyper crème de cacao
2 oz. light cream

Shake and serve up in a martini glass.

PIXIE STICK

2 oz. DeKuyper Pucker Cheri-Beri
2 oz. sweet & sour mix
splash lemon-lime soda

Serve as a mixed drink.

POISON APPLE

1/4 oz. Knob Creek bourbon
1/4 oz. DeKuyper Pucker sour apple
1/4 oz. Vox vodka
1/4 oz. Bacardi rum
1/4 oz. DeKuyper crème de banana
1 oz. sweet & sour mix

Shake and serve in a tall glass.

POISON APPLE II

1 1/4 parts DeKuyper Pucker sour apple
3/4 part DeKuyper Thrilla Vanilla
1 part Rose's grenadine

Pour over ice in a tall glass. Fill with lemon-lime soda.

POISON RED APPLE

1/2 oz. Knob Creek bourbon
1/2 oz. DeKuyper Pucker sour apple
1/2 oz. Vox vodka
1/2 oz. Bacardi rum
1/2 oz. DeKuyper crème de banana
2 oz. sweet & sour mix

Shake with ice and pour in a tall glass. Top with cranberry juice.

POLO

1 1/4 oz. Bombay Sapphire gin
2 oz. grapefruit juice
2 oz. orange juice

In a tall glass with ice, fill with half grapefruit juice and half orange juice.

POUSSE-CAFÈ STANDISH

1/2 oz. Rose's grenadine
1/2 oz. DeKuyper white crème de menthe
1/2 oz. Galliano
1/2 oz. kummel
1/2 oz. Hennessy cognac

Layer this drink in the order listed. Start with Rose's grenadine on the bottom and finish with Hennessy cognac on top.

PRAIRIE FIRE

1 1/2 oz. Jose Cuervo tequila
2 or 3 drops Tabasco sauce

Combine in a shot glass.

PRESBYTERIAN

2 oz. Knob Creek bourbon
ginger ale
club soda

Pour the Knob Creek bourbon into a chilled highball glass. Add ice cubes. Top off the glass with equal parts of ginger ale and soda.

PRESIDENTE

1/4 oz. Martini & Rossi dry vermouth
3/4 oz. Martini & Rossi Rosso vermouth
1 1/2 oz. Bacardi light rum
splash Rose's grenadine

Mix with ice and serve.

PRINCE EDWARD

1/2 oz. Drambuie
1 oz. Dewar's scotch
1/2 oz. Lillet Blanc
orange slice

Combine all ingredients, except orange slice, with cracked ice in a cocktail shaker. Shake well and pour into a chilled old-fashioned glass. Garnish with an orange slice.

PROPAGANDA

5 strawberries, chopped
2 tsp. fine sugar
3/4 oz. sugar syrup
ice
1 oz. Vox vodka
1 oz. Chambord

Shake. Serve on rocks.

PRIVILEGE & GINGER

1 oz. Hennessy Privilege

Serve over ice in a snifter, fill with ginger ale.

PUCKER APPLE-ADE

1 shot DeKuyper Pucker sour apple

Fill with lemonade. Serve on the rocks in a tall glass.

PUCKER CHERI-ADE

1 shot DeKuyper Pucker Cheri-Beri

Fill with lemonade; serve on the rocks in a tall glass.

PUCKER PANDEMONIUM FREEZE

2 oz. DeKuyper Pucker sour apple
1 oz. vanilla ice cream

Blend.

PUCKER PANDEMONIUM FREEZE II

2 oz. DeKuyper Pucker Cheri-Beri
1 oz. vanilla ice cream

Blend.

PUCKER UP

1 oz. DeKuyper Pucker sour apple

Fill glass with lemon-lime soda and ice.

PUCKERED DISASTER

Equal parts:
    1 oz. Avalanche Blue
    1/2 oz. After Shock liqueur
    1 oz. DeKuyper Pucker sour apple

Shake with ice.

PUCKERED MADRAS

1 oz. DeKuyper Pucker sour apple
1 oz. Vox vodka
1 oz. cranberry juice
1 oz. orange juice

Shake with ice.

PUCKERED UP RUSSIAN

2 parts DeKuyper Pucker sour apple
1 part Vox vodka (frozen)

Combine and serve as a shot.

PUCKERITA

1/2 oz. DeKuyper Pucker Cheri-Beri
1 oz. Jose Cuervo tequila
sweet & sour mix
dash lime juice

Shake with ice; serve in a tall glass.

PULCO

2 oz. Jose Cuervo 1800 tequila
1/2 oz. Cointreau
1 1/2 oz. lime juice

Combine over ice.

PUNCH IN THE PANTS

1 oz. Bacardi O
1 oz. Bacardi Limón
splash Cointreau
splash sweet & sour mix
3 oz. orange soda

Blend with ice.

PURPLE HAZE

1 oz. Chambord
1 oz. Vox vodka
1 oz. cranberry juice or sweet & sour mix

Combine in a shot glass.

PURPLE HAZE MARTINI COCKTAIL

2 oz. Bacardi O
2 oz. lemonade
1/4 oz. Rose's grenadine
1/2 oz. DeKuyper blue curacao

Shake with ice; strain and serve in a chilled martini glass; garnish with an orange slice.

PURPLE HOOTER

1/2 oz. Vox vodka
1/2 oz. Chambord
1/2 oz. cranberry juice
splash club soda

Shake and strain Vox vodka, Chambord, and cranberry juice. Top with a splash of club soda.

PURPLE ORCHID

1 part DeKuyper white crème de cacao
1 part DeKuyper blackberry brandy
1 part cream

Combine in a shot glass.

PURPLE PASSION

1 1/4 oz. Vox vodka
2 oz. grapefruit juice
2 oz. grape juice

Combine ingredients and stir. Serve in a collins glass.

QUEEN ELIZABETH MARTINI

1 1/2 oz. Bombay Sapphire gin
splash Martini & Rossi extra dry vermouth
splash Benedictine

Stir in a cocktail glass. Strain and serve straight up or on the rocks. Add a lemon twist or olives.

RACER'S EDGE

1 1/2 oz. Bacardi light rum
1/4 oz. DeKuyper green crème de menthe
grapefruit juice

Pour Bacardi into a glass half filled with ice. Fill with grapefruit juice and float crème de menthe.

RAIN DROP

2 oz. Vox vodka
1 oz. lemon juice
sugar

Shake. Serve in a sugarcoated, chilled cocktail glass with a squeeze of lemon.

RAMOS FIZZ

1 1/2 oz. Bombay Sapphire gin
1 tbs. powdered sugar
3–4 drops orange-flower
water
juice 1/2 lime
juice 1/2 lemon
1 egg white
1 1/2 oz. cream
seltzer
2 drops vanilla extract

Mix ingredients in the order given. Add crushed ice. Shake. Strain into a tall glass.

RASMOPOLITAN

1 1/4 parts Vox raspberry vodka
1/2 part Cointreau
1 part cranberry juice
squeeze fresh lime juice

Mix in a shaker half-filled with ice. Pour into a chilled martini glass. Garnish with fresh raspberries or a lime peel.

RASPBERRY BREEZE

1 part Vox raspberry vodka
2 parts cranberry juice
2 parts grapefruit juice

Shake all ingredients with ice and pour into a martini glass.

RASPBERRY DELIGHT

3/4 oz. Drambuie
3/4 oz. Chambord
1/2 oz. DeKuyper coffee liqueur
fresh raspberries
1 scoop ice cream

Blend.

RASPBERRY FLIRTINI

1 part Vox raspberry vodka
1/2 part Chambord
1 part champagne (float)

Mix vodka and Chambord in a shaker half filled with ice. Pour into a champagne flute and top with champagne. Garnish with fresh raspberries.

RASPBERRY HONEY NUTS

1 oz. honey walnut cream liqueur
1 oz. Chambord
2 oz. half-and-half
5 raspberries

Shake and serve in a rocks glass. Top with raspberries.

RASPBERRY KIR

1 oz. Vox raspberry vodka
1/4 oz. champagne

In a chilled fluted champagne glass, garnish with a raspberry.

RASPBERRY MARGARITA

2 1/2oz. Bacardi Razz
1 oz. Cointreau
1/2 oz. Rose's lime juice
1 oz. sweet & sour mix
splash cranberry juice

Pour over ice into a rocks glass. Garnish with a lime.

Matthew "Woody" Woodburn
Sinibar
Chicago, IL

RASPBERRY MARTINI

2 parts Vox raspberry vodka
1/4 part Chambord
6 fresh raspberries

Muddle raspberries with vodka and Chambord. Shake with ice and strain into a glass.

RASPBERRY MINT DAIQUIRI

1 1/2 oz. Bacardi light rum
1/2 oz. cranberry juice
2 oz. sweet & sour mix
1 oz. raspberry mint puree
1/2 oz. Chambord

Shake or blend; serve in a tall glass.

RASPBERRY SPRITZER

1 1/4 parts Vox raspberry vodka
3/4 part Chambord
3 parts lemon-lime soda

Combine Vox raspberry vodka and lemon-lime soda in a tall glass filled with ice. Add Chambord, letting it gently sink to the bottom. Garnish with a fresh raspberry.

RASPBERRY TRUFFLE

1 1/2 parts Vox raspberry vodka
1 part DeKuyper white crème de cacao
1/2 part Chambord
3/4 part half-and-half

Mix in a shaker half-filled with ice. Pour into a martini glass rimmed with cocoa.

RAZZ-MA-TAZZ

1 1/2 oz. Vox vodka
1/2 oz. Chambord
1 1/2 oz. club soda

Serve over ice in a tall glass, chilled.

RAZZ LEMONADE

8 oz. lemonade
1 oz. Monin raspberry syrup
1 1/4 oz. Bacardi Razz rum

Fill a 16 oz. glass mug with ice. Add ingredients in order of listing. Stir well to blend. Serve with a lemon wedge.

RED HEADED MEXICAN

1 1/4 oz. Jose Cuervo Clásico
4 oz. lemon-lime soda
1/4 oz. cranberry juice

Serve in a tall glass.

RED HOT MAMA

1 1/4 oz. Bacardi rum
4 oz. cranberry juice
2 oz. club soda

Combine over ice.

RED RAIDER

1 oz. Knob Creek bourbon
1/2 oz. Cointreau
1 oz. lemon juice
dash grenadine

Shake with ice and strain into a tall glass.

RED REBEL

1 part Jose Cuervo Clásico
4 parts lemon-lime soda
splash cranberry juice

*Combine tequila and lemon-lime soda in a rocks glass
with ice. Stir. Add splash of cranberry juice. Garnish with
a lemon or orange peel.*

ROAD KILL

1 part Tullamore Dew Irish whiskey
1 part Knob Creek bourbon
1 part Bacardi rum (151-proof)

Combine in a shot glass.

ROB ROY

2 oz. Dewar's White Label scotch
dash Martini & Rossi Rosso or dry vermouth

Stir over ice and strain. You can also serve over ice.

ROOTY-TOOTY

1 1/4 oz. DeKuyper Old Tavern root beer
   schnapps
3 oz. orange juice

Mix with ice in a blender; serve over ice in an on-the-rocks glass.

ROYAL BOMBAY SAPPHIRE GIN FIZZ

2 oz. Bombay Sapphire gin
1/2 oz. Cointreau
1 oz. sweet & sour mix
1 oz. club soda

Fill mixing glass with ice and all ingredients except club soda. Shake and strain into a chilled glass. Fill with club soda.

RUBY SLIPPER MARTINI

2 oz. Bombay Sapphire gin
1/4 oz. Cointreau
1–2 splashes Rose's grenadine
1 dash DeKuyper peppermint schnapps

Garnish with a mint leaf. (Set it on the edge of the drink and let it stick out.)

RUDE COSMOPOLITAN

1 part Jose Cuervo Clásico
1/4 part Cointreau
1 part cranberry juice
juice from a whole lime

Shake all ingredients with ice. Strain into a chilled cocktail glass. Garnish with an orange peel.

RUE L'ORANGE MARTINI COCKTAIL

1 1/2 oz. Bacardi O
1 oz. Lillet Blanc
1 1/4 oz. cranberry juice
splash sweet & sour mix

Shake; strain and serve in a chilled martini glass; garnish with an orange twist.

RUM & COKE

1 1/2 oz. Bacardi light rum
3 oz. cola

Stir ingredients with ice.

RUSTY NAIL

1/2 oz. Drambuie
1 1/2 oz. Dewar's scotch

Serve on the rocks.

S.O.S.

3 parts Bacardi O
1 part Chambord
2 parts sweet & sour
1 part cranberry juice

Shake all ingredients with ice and strain into a shot glass.

SA PUCKER SUCKER

1/2 oz. DeKuyper Pucker sour apple
1/2 oz. DeKuyper coffee liqueur
1/2 oz. orange juice

Combine; serve as shot.

SAKE O MARTINI COCKTAIL

2 oz. Bacardi O
1/4 oz. sake
1/4 oz. cranberry juice

Shake with ice; strain into a chilled martini glass.

SALT LICK

1 1/4 oz. Vox vodka
2 oz. bitter lemon soda
2 oz. grapefruit juice

Pour over ice in a salt-rimmed wine glass.

SALTY DOG

1 1/4 oz. Bombay Sapphire gin
grapefruit juice
salt

Wet rim of a tall glass with juice or water and dip into salt to coat (optional). Pour Bombay over ice; fill with grapefruit juice and stir.

SANTA FE MAGGIE

1 1/4 oz. Jose Cuervo gold tequila
1/2 oz. Cointreau
2 oz. sweet & sour mix
2 oz. cranberry juice

Combine ingredients over ice and garnish with a lime wedge.

SAPLING

1 oz. Laird's applejack
1 oz. Cointreau
1 oz. lime juice

Shake well with ice; strain into a tall glass filled with shaved ice. Garnish with a sprig of mint.

SAPPHIRE & TONIC

2 oz. Bombay Sapphire tonic
squeeze lime

In a tall glass filled with ice, add Bombay Sapphire and fill with tonic. Add a squeeze of lime.

SAPPHIRE MARTINI

2 oz. Bombay Sapphire gin
1/2 oz. Martini & Rossi dry vermouth

Garnish with an olive.

SAPPHIRE ROSE

2 oz. Bombay Sapphire gin
fresh grapefruit juice
sugar syrup
maraschino liqueur

Combine in a tall glass.

SAPPHIRE SOUR

2 oz. Bombay Sapphire gin
juice of 1/2 lemon
1/2 tsp. powdered sugar

Mix ingredients with cracked ice in shaker; strain into a martini glass.

SATIN ROUGE MARTINI COCKTAIL

1 1/4 oz. Bacardi O
1/2 oz. Tropico liqueur
1/4 oz. cherry juice
1/2 oz. pineapple juice

Serve in a chilled glass; garnish with a lemon twist.

SCARLETT KISS

Mix Drambuie with cranberry juice and serve over ice in a tall glass.

SCARLETT O'HARA

1 1/2 oz. Southern Comfort
3 oz. cranberry juice

Combine with ice and stir.

SCHNAPPY SHILLELAGH

2 parts Carolans Irish cream
1 part DeKuyper peppermint schnapps

Stir well over ice.

SCORPION

1/2 part Vox vodka
1/2 part DeKuyper blackberry brandy
1 part Rose's grenadine

Combine in a shot glass.

SCOTCH 'N' SODA

2 oz. Dewar's White Label scotch
3 oz. club soda

Stir with ice.

SCOTCH SMOOTHIE

1 oz. Coco Lopez cream of coconut
1 1/4 oz. Dewar's White Label scotch
1/2 oz. Carolans Irish cream
1/2 oz. DeKuyper crème de almond liqueur
2 scoops vanilla ice cream

Blend.

SCOTCH SOUR

1 1/4 oz. Dewar's White Label scotch
1 oz. lemon juice
1 tsp. sugar

Stir in a mixing glass and pour into a rocks glass with ice. Garnish with a cherry and an orange slice.

SCOTTISH ICED TEA

One part Drambuie in a tall glass of freshly brewed unsweetened iced tea, garnished with lemon or a sprig of mint.

SCOTTY DOG

2 oz. Dewar's White Label scotch
1 1/2 oz. Rose's lime juice

Shake with ice and strain into a glass. Garnish with a slice of lime.

SCREAMING SOUR APPLES

1 1/4 oz. Vox vodka
3/4 oz. DeKuyper Pucker sour apple
2 1/2 oz. sweet & sour mix

Shake and serve in a tall glass.

SCREWDRIVER

1 1/4 oz. Vox vodka
4 oz. orange juice

Add Vox vodka to a tall glass with ice and fill with orange juice.

SCREWY APPLE

1 1/4 oz. DeKuyper Pucker sour apple
3 oz. orange juice

Serve in a tall glass.

SEA BREEZE

2 oz. Vox vodka
2 oz. cranberry juice
2 oz. grapefruit juice

Shake ingredients with ice and strain into an ice-filled glass.

SEA DIPPER

1 1/2 oz. Bacardi light rum
1 oz. pineapple juice
1/4 oz. Rose's lime juice
1 tsp. powdered sugar

Shake with ice and serve over ice.

SECRET PLACE

1 1/2 oz. Bacardi dark rum
1/2 oz. DeKuyper cherry brandy
2 tsp. DeKuyper dark crème de cacao
4 oz. cold coffee

Stir with crushed ice and serve in a tall glass.

SEE-THRU

2 oz. Bombay Sapphire gin

Pour over lots of ice.

SEX ON THE BEACH

3/4 oz. Chambord
3/4 oz. DeKuyper melon liqueur
2 oz. pineapple juice
splash cranberry juice

Combine in a mixing glass. Shake or stir. Pour in a shot glass. You can also serve this one over ice in a rocks glass.

SEX ON THE BEACH (SOUTHERN STYLE)

1/2 oz. DeKuyper Pucker sour apple
1/2 oz. DeKuyper Peachtree schnapps
1/2 oz. cranberry juice
1/2 oz. pineapple juice

Shake or stir. Pour in a shot glass.

SHAMROCK COCKTAIL

1 1/2 oz. Tullamore Dew Irish whiskey
1/2 oz. Martini & Rossi dry vermouth
1/4 oz. DeKuyper green crème de menthe

Stir well with cracked ice and strain or serve over ice. Garnish with an olive.

SHAMROCK COCKTAIL II

1 1/2 oz. Tullamore Dew Irish whiskey
3/4 oz. DeKuyper green crème de menthe
4 oz. vanilla ice cream

Blend. Pour into a chilled wine goblet.

SHETLAND PONY

1 1/2 oz. Dewar's scotch
3/4 oz. Irish Mist
dash orange bitters

Mix all ingredients with cracked ice and strain into a chilled cocktail glass. You can also serve this drink over ice.

SHORE BREEZE

1 1/2 oz. Bacardi light rum
3 oz. pineapple juice
2 oz. cranberry juice
2 dashes Angostura

Shake with ice and serve in a rocks glass.

SHOOTER, SLAMMER, OR MUPPET

1 part Jose Cuervo Especial
1 part lemon-lime soda

Pour Jose Cuervo Especial and lemon-lime soda into a shot glass. Hold the filled glass with your palm firmly covering the top of the glass so the liquid does not spill out when you slam it onto the table, hard. After slamming, immediately shoot it all at once.

SIBERIAN SUNRISE

1 1/2 oz. Vox vodka
4 oz. grapefruit juice
1/2 oz. Cointreau

Mix all ingredients with cracked ice in a shaker or blend.

SICILIAN KISS

2 parts Southern Comfort
1 part Disaronno amaretto

Pour over crushed ice in short glasses; stir.

SIDECAR

1 1/2 oz. Hennessy VS
3/4 oz. Cointreau
3/4 tsp. fresh lemon juice

Combine all ingredients in a shaker and shake vigorously. Strain into a chilled cocktail glass, with a sugarcoated rim.

SIDECAR IN BOMBAY

1 1/2 oz. Bombay Sapphire gin
1/4 oz. Cointreau
1/4 oz. lemon juice

Shake with ice and serve on the rocks or up in a sugar-rimmed glass.

SIESTA

1 1/2 oz. Jose Cuervo tequila
3/4 oz. lime juice
1/2 oz. Bombay Sapphire gin

Shake with ice and strain into a chilled cocktail glass.

SILK PANTIES

1 part Vox vodka
1 part DeKuyper Peachtree schnapps

Combine in a shot glass.

Sandra Gutierrez
Chicago, IL

SILVER BULLET MARTINI

1 1/2 oz. Vox vodka
dash Martini & Rossi
extra dry vermouth
splash Dewar's scotch

Stir the first two ingredients gently over ice and strain.
Float Dewar's on top.

SIMPLY BONKERS

1 oz. Chambord
1 oz. Bacardi rum
1 oz. cream

Combine in a shot glass.

SINGAPORE SLING

1 oz. Bombay Sapphire gin
1/2 oz. DeKuyper cherry brandy
3 dashes Benedictine
dash Rose's grenadine
1/2 oz. sweetened lemon mix
club soda

Shake first five ingredients and pour into a tall glass. Top with club soda.

SLIM JIM

1 1/4 oz. Vox vodka
3 oz. diet soda

In a highball glass with ice, fill with diet soda. Garnish with a lemon or lime slice.

SLIM BOMBAY SAPPHIRE GIN

1 1/2 oz. Bombay Sapphire gin
2 oz. diet soda

Fill a tall glass with ice and your favorite diet soda.

SLOE BOMBAY SAPPHIRE GIN FIZZ

1 oz. DeKuyper sloe gin
1 oz. Bombay Sapphire gin
1 1/2 oz. sweet & sour mix
club soda

Shake, pour with ice into 12 oz. fizz glass, and fill with soda. Add a maraschino cherry garnish.

SLOE BOMBAY SAPPHIRE GIN FIZZ II

1 1/2 oz. Bombay Sapphire gin
3 oz. sweetened lemon mix
club soda

Shake Bombay Sapphire gin and lemon mix and pour into a glass. Top with club soda.

SMOOTH PINK LEMONADE

1 1/2 oz. Vox vodka
2 oz. cranberry juice
2 oz. sweet & sour mix
1/2 oz. lemon-lime soda

Shake and serve in a tall glass over ice.

SNOW DROP

1/4 oz. Cointreau
1/4 oz. Liquore Galliano
1/4 oz. Vox vodka
1/4 oz. DeKuyper white crème de cacao
1 oz. cream

Shake with ice and strain.

SOGGY CHERRY

2 oz. DeKuyper Pucker Cheri-Beri
3 slightly crushed maraschino cherries

Fill with soda.

SOL-A-RITA

1 1/4 oz. Jose Cuervo gold tequila
3/4 oz. Cointreau
1 1/2 oz. orange juice
2 dashes Rose's grenadine

Shake or blend. Serve straight up or on the rocks.

SOPHISTICATE

1 oz. Bacardi O
1/2 oz. DeKuyper melon liqueur
1/2 oz. lemon-lime soda
1/2 oz. cranberry juice

Serve over ice. Garnish with melon, strawberry, and sugarcoated orange.

SOUR APPLE MARGARITA

2 oz. DeKuyper Pucker sour apple
1 oz. Jose Cuervo tequila
1/2 oz. lime juice
3 oz. sweet & sour mix

Shake or blend. Serve in salt-rimmed glass.

SOUR APPLE PUCKER DRIVER

Fill tall glass with ice and orange juice. Pour DeKuyper Pucker sour apple on top. Let filter down through the juice, stir.

SOUR APPLE PUCKER POPSICLE

2 oz. DeKuyper Pucker sour apple
1 cup vanilla ice cream

Blend.

SOUR APPLE SNOW CONES

2 oz. DeKuyper Pucker sour apple

Served over crushed ice.

SOUR APPLE SPORTIER

1 1/2 oz. DeKuyper Pucker sour apple
1/2 oz. Vox vodka
2 oz. lemon-lime soda

Stir with ice in a tall glass.

SOUR APPLE SPRITZER

1 1/2 oz. DeKuyper Pucker sour apple
1/2 oz. Vox vodka
2 oz. club soda

Stir with ice in a tall glass. Top with club soda.

SOUR APPLETINI

Equal parts:
    DeKuyper Pucker sour apple
    Vox vodka
    splash sweet & sour mix

Chill, strain, serve in a martini glass. Garnish with an apple slice.

SOUR KISSES MARTINI

1 1/2 oz. Bombay Sapphire gin
dash Martini & Rossi extra dry vermouth
1/2 oz. DeKuyper Pucker sour apple

Stir. Strain into a martini glass.

SOUTH FORK COFFEE

1 1/2 oz. Knob Creek bourbon
1/2 oz. DeKuyper dark crème de cacao
3 oz. coffee

Add Knob Creek bourbon and DeKuyper dark crème de cacao to coffee.

SOUTHERN ALEXANDER

1 1/2 oz. Southern Comfort
1 1/2 oz. DeKuyper dark crème de cacao
1/2 oz. cream
1 cup ice

Blend.

SOUTHERN FROST

1 1/2 oz. Southern Comfort
2 oz. cranberry juice
2 oz. ginger ale

Fill a tall glass with ice. Add all ingredients and stir.

SOUTHERN LADY

2 oz. Knob Creek bourbon
1/2 oz. Southern Comfort
1/2 oz. DeKuyper crème de almond
3 oz. pineapple juice
1 oz. lime juice
2 oz. lemon-lime soda

Shake first four ingredients with ice and strain into a hurricane glass half-filled with ice. Fill with soda. Top with lime juice. Garnish with a pineapple wheel and a maraschino cherry.

SOUTHERN PEACH

1 3/4 oz. Knob Creek bourbon
1 oz. DeKuyper Peachtree schnapps
1/8 oz. grenadine
2 oz. orange juice
2 oz. sweet & sour mix

Fill a parfait or hurricane glass with ice. Pour grenadine over ice; add bourbon. Pour orange juice, sour mix, and schnapps and shake. Garnish with a peach slice.

SOUTHERN PINK FLAMINGO

2 oz. Southern Comfort
1/2 oz. Bacardi rum
2 oz. pineapple juice
splash Rose's grenadine
1 oz. lemon juice

Shake and serve over ice.

SOUTHERN SHAG

1 1/2 oz. Southern Comfort
2 oz. cranberry juice
1/2 oz. orange juice

Stir and garnish with a lime wedge.

SOUTHERN TRADITIONAL MARGARITA

1 1/2 oz. Jose Cuervo gold tequila
5/8 oz. Southern Comfort
5 oz. sweet & sour mix
1/2 oz. fresh lime juice

Combine in a tall glass over ice. Garnish with a lime wedge.

SPANISH MARTINI

1 1/2 oz. Bombay Sapphire gin
1/2 oz. Spanish Sherry

Shake with ice and strain into a chilled martini glass. Garnish with a lemon twist.

SPEARAMISTY

1 oz. Irish Mist
1/4 oz. DeKuyper spearmint schnapps

Stir ingredients and serve straight up or over ice.

SPIKE

1 1/2 oz. Jose Cuervo gold tequila
4 oz. grapefruit juice

Combine in a highball glass.

SPIRITED COFFEE LOPEZ

1/2 oz. Coco Lopez cream of coconut
8 oz. hot coffee
1/2 oz. Tullamore Dew Irish whiskey

Serve in coffee mug. Add whipped cream as desired.

SPRING FLING

Equal parts:
    DeKuyper Pucker Cheri-Beri
    Grape Pucker
    Mad Melon
    San Tropique

Combine over ice with orange juice, pineapple juice, and top with cranberry juice; shake and serve.

SPRITZER

3 oz. dry white wine
club soda

Pour wine in a glass and fill with soda. Garnish with a lemon twist.

ST. PATRICK'S DAY COCKTAIL

3/4 oz. Tullamore Dew Irish whiskey
3/4 oz. DeKuyper green crème de menthe
3/4 oz. green Chartreuse
dash Angostura bitters

Stir. Serve over ice.

STAIRCASE

1/4 oz. Drambuie
1 oz. Dewar's scotch
1/4 oz. Martini & Rossi dry vermouth
1/4 oz. Martini & Rossi Rosso vermouth

Serve in a rocks glass with ice.

STEAMBOAT SPECIAL

1/4 oz. Cointreau
1 oz. Dewar's scotch

Float Cointreau over Dewar's scotch in a shot glass.

STEEPLE JACK

1 oz. Laird's applejack
2 oz. Rose's lime juice

Mix over ice in a short glass. Garnish with a lime wedge.

STILETTO

1 1/2 oz. Knob Creek bourbon
1 oz. Disaronno amaretto
juice of 1/2 lemon

Shake with ice. Pour into a glass over ice cubes.

STINGER

2 oz. Hennessy cognac
3/4 oz. DeKuyper white crème de menthe

Shake with ice and strain into a chilled cocktail glass or brandy snifter.

STOPLIGHT

2 oz. DeKuyper sloe gin
2 oz. Bombay Sapphire gin
1 oz. lemon juice
1 scoop crushed ice
1 maraschino cherry

Shake with ice. Strain the mixture into a chilled cocktail glass. Garnish with a maraschino cherry.

SUBMARINE

Jose Cuervo Especial
beer
All the time in the world

Fill a shot glass with Jose Cuervo Especial. Very slowly put the shot upside down inside a beer mug, making sure the Cuervo stays inside the shot glass. Slowly fill the mug with beer. Try not to mix the Cuervo with the beer. Drink it all in one shot.

SUNBURST

1 1/4 oz. Vox vodka
dash Cointreau
2 oz. grapefruit juice

Serve in a rocks glass over ice. Add a dash of Cointreau.

SUNSET MARTINI COCKTAIL

1 1/2 oz. Bacardi O
1/2 oz. Tropico liqueur
3 oz. lemonade

Shake with ice and strain into a sugar-rimmed martini glass. Float Tropico liqueur on top.

SUNSET PUNCH

1 1/2 oz. Bacardi light rum
4 oz. orange juice
1/2 oz. Rose's lime juice
1/2 oz. Rose's grenadine

Shake Bacardi light rum, orange juice, and Rose's lime juice. Pour into a tall glass filled with ice. Spoon in Rose's grenadine.

SUPER O MARTINI COCKTAIL

2 oz. Bacardi O
1 oz. Tropico liqueur
1/4 oz. Bombay Sapphire gin
1/4 oz. Cointreau

Shake; serve in a chilled glass with an orange garnish.

SUPER MARTINI COCKTAIL

1 oz. Bacardi O
1/4 oz. Rose's grenadine
1/4 oz. orange juice

Shake with ice; strain into a chilled martini glass.

SURE BOMBAY SAPPHIRE GIN FIZZ

2 oz. Bombay Sapphire gin
2 oz. sweetened lemon mix
club soda

Shake with ice. Serve in a tall glass filled with ice. Top with club soda.

SWAMP WATER

3/4 oz. Cointreau
3/4 oz. green Chartreuse
1/2 oz. pineapple juice

Shake with ice and strain.

SWEET & SOUR APPLETINI

1 oz. DeKuyper Pucker sour apple
1 oz. Vox vodka
splash sweet & sour mix

Shake with ice, strain, and serve in a chilled martini glass.

SWEET TART

1 oz. Vox vodka
1/4 oz. Chambord
1/4 oz. Rose's lime juice
1/4 oz. pineapple juice

Shake with ice and strain into a shot glass.

SWEET MARTINI

2 oz. Bombay Sapphire gin
3/4 oz. Martini & Rossi Rosso vermouth

Stir with ice and serve over rocks or strain into a chilled martini glass. Garnish with an orange twist.

SWEETEST TABOO

1 oz. Campari
1 oz. Cointreau
1 1/2 oz. Bombay Sapphire gin
orange juice

Pour Campari, Cointreau, and Bombay Sapphire gin into a glass with ice. Fill with orange juice. Stir.

TANGO MARTINI COCKTAIL

2 oz. Bacardi O
1/2 oz. Chambord
1/2 oz. Cointreau
1 oz. pineapple juice
splash cranberry juice

Shake with ice; strain into a chilled martini glass.
Squeeze an orange in the bottom of the glass; garnish
with an orange twist.

TARZAN O'REILLY

1 oz. Carolans Irish cream
1 oz. Vox vodka
1 oz. DeKuyper crème de banana

Stir. Serve on the rocks.

TEA WITH LOVE

2 oz. Disaronno amaretto
6 oz. hot tea

Top with chilled whipped cream. Serve in a mug.

TEQUADOR

1 1/2 oz. Jose Cuervo tequila
2 oz. pineapple juice
dash Rose's lime juice
Rose's grenadine

Shake the first three ingredients with crushed ice. Strain. Add a few drops of Rose's grenadine.

TEQUILA GIMLET

1 1/2 oz. Jose Cuervo tequila
1 1/2 oz. Rose's lime juice

Blend Cuervo and lime juice with crushed ice and pour into a glass. Garnish with a lime wheel or green cherry.

TEQUILA JULEP

1 1/4 oz. Jose Cuervo tequila
1 tsp. superfine sugar
2 sprigs fresh mint
club soda

Crush three mint leaves with sugar in a chilled highball glass and fill with ice. Add Cuervo and top with club soda. Garnish with a sprig of mint.

TEQUILA SUNRISE

1 1/2 oz. Jose Cuervo tequila
1/2 oz. Rose's grenadine
orange juice

Pour Rose's grenadine into a tall glass first. Then add Cuervo and fill with ice and orange juice. Garnish with an orange slice.

TEQUILA TEASER

1 1/2 oz. Jose Cuervo tequila
1/2 oz. Cointreau
1 1/2 oz. orange juice
1/2 oz. grapefruit juice

Pour ingredients into a tall glass filled with ice.

TEQUINA

2 oz. Jose Cuervo tequila
1/2 oz. Martini & Rossi dry vermouth

Stir Cuervo and vermouth with ice in a mixing glass until chilled. Strain into a chilled cocktail glass and garnish with a lemon twist.

THE BACARDI FIZZLE

1 oz. Bacardi Razz
splash Cointreau
1 1/2 oz. cranberry juice

Shake ingredients with ice. Pour into a tall glass. Top with lemon-lime soda.

THE BIG APPLE

1 1/2 oz. DeKuyper Pucker sour apple
1/2 oz. Rose's grenadine
1/2 oz. lemon juice

Serve over ice.

THE BOMB

Equal parts:
    DeKuyper Pucker grape
    DeKuyper Pucker Cheri-Beri
    DeKuyper Pucker sour apple
    DeKuyper BluesBerry
    DeKuyper Mad Melon
    Vox vodka
    cranberry juice

Shake and serve in a tall glass or strain into a shot glass.

THE CUERVO SHOT

1 oz. Jose Cuervo Especial
pinch salt
lime wedge

Pour Jose Cuervo Especial into a shot glass. Lick the skin between your thumb and forefinger and sprinkle salt on the moist skin. Drink the tequila (all at once, quickly), lick the salt and suck on the lime.

THE LONDON MARTINI

2 oz. Bombay Sapphire gin
1/2 oz. Martini & Rossi Rosso vermouth
1/2 oz. DeKuyper blue curacao
splash pineapple juice

Mix all ingredients with cracked ice in shaker; strain into a martini glass.

THE S.O.S.

3 parts Bacardi O
1 part Chambord
2 parts sweet & sour mix
1 part cranberry juice

Shake all ingredients with ice and strain into a shot glass.

THOROUGHBRED COOLER

1 oz. Knob Creek bourbon
1 oz. orange juice
dash Rose's grenadine
lemon-lime soda

Pour all ingredients over ice in a highball glass. Fill with lemon-lime soda and stir. Add dash of grenadine; garnish with an orange wedge.

TIDAL WAVE

1 1/2 oz. Laird's applejack
4 oz. orange juice
splash cranberry juice

Pour Laird's applejack over ice in a tall glass. Add orange juice and a splash of cranberry juice. Garnish with a slice of orange.

TIPPERARY COCKTAIL

3/4 oz. Tullamore Dew Irish whiskey
3/4 oz. green Chartreuse
3/4 oz. Martini & Rossi dry vermouth

Stir well with cracked ice and strain into a cocktail glass.

TO THE MOON

1 oz. Carolans Irish cream
1 oz. Disaronno amaretto
1/2 oz. DeKuyper coffee liqueur
1/4 oz. Bacardi rum (151-proof)

Serve in a shot glass.

TOASTED ALMOND

1 oz. DeKuyper coffee liqueur
1/2 oz. Disaronno amaretto
1 oz. cream or milk

Pour over ice and stir.

TOASTED IRISHMAN

1 part Irish Mist
1 part DeKuyper coffee liqueur
1 part Disaronno amaretto

Shake with ice and serve on the rocks.

TOM & JERRY

1 oz. Bacardi light rum
1/4 oz. Bacardi Select rum
1 egg
1 tsp. sugar

Separate yolk from white of egg and beat each separately. When white is fairly stiff, add sugar and beat to a stiff froth, combine white and yolk. Put rums in a mug, add boiling water, 1 tablespoon of egg mixture, and sprinkle with nutmeg.

TOM COLLINS

2 oz. Bombay Sapphire gin
2 oz. sweetened lemon mix
club soda

Shake Bombay and lemon mix with ice; fill a tall glass. Add club soda. Garnish with a maraschino cherry and orange slice.

TOPAZ MARTINI

1 3/4 oz. Bacardi Limón
1/4 oz. Martini & Rossi extra dry vermouth
splash DeKuyper blue curacao

Combine in a cocktail glass.

Heart and Soul
San Francisco, CA

TRAIL BLAZE

1 oz. Drambuie
1 oz. Chambord
1 oz. sweet & sour mix

Shake with ice. Serve over ice.

TRANSFUSION

1 1/4 oz. Vox vodka
3 oz. grape juice

In a tall glass with ice, fill with grape juice. Top with club soda (optional).

TROPICAL APPLE PIE

1 1/4 oz. DeKuyper Pucker sour apple
2 scoops vanilla ice cream
1/4 oz. scoop ice
2 wedges, cored apple
2 oz. Coco Lopez cream of coconut

Blend. Serve in a tall glass.

TROPICAL APPLE PUNCH

1 1/2 oz. DeKuyper Pucker sour apple
1/2 oz. DeKuyper San Tropique
3 oz. cranberry juice
3 oz. orange juice

Serve in a tall glass.

TROPICAL APPLE PUNCH II

1 1/2 oz. DeKuyper Pucker sour apple
1/2 oz. Bacardi Còco
3 oz. cranberry juice
3 oz. orange juice

Serve in a tall glass.

TROPICAL BREEZE

1 oz. Coco Lopez cream of coconut
2 oz. orange juice
1 oz. Bacardi rum
1/2 oz. DeKuyper crème de banana

Blend. Garnish with a pineapple slice.

TROPICAL RENDEZVOUS

2 parts DeKuyper Tropical pineapple schnapps
1 part DeKuyper Peachtree schnapps

Fill with lemon-lime soda over ice in tall glass.

TROPICAL STORM

1 1/2 oz. Cointreau
1 1/2 oz. DeKuyper crème de banana liqueur
1 oz. lime or lemon juice
mint leaves
cherry

Shake lime (or lemon juice), DeKuyper banana liqueur, and Cointreau with ice. Strain into a tumbler glass full of ice. Stir. Garnish with mint leaves, a maraschino cherry, and a lime slice.

TRUE BLUE

1/2 part Jose Cuervo Especial
1/2 part Vox vodka
1/2 part DeKuyper blue curacao

Pour all ingredients into a cocktail shaker with crushed ice and shake well. Strain into a chilled shot glass.

TULLAMORE DEW HOT IRISH TEA

1 1/2 oz. Tullamore Dew Irish whiskey
4 oz. hot tea

In a mug stir the ingredients well. Add a cinnamon stick.

TULLAMORE DEW IRISH COOLER

1 jigger Tullamore Dew Irish whiskey
1 pint club soda
dash Angostura bitters
1 lemon rind

Serve in a tall glass.

TUSCAN RED SANGRIA

1 750ml bottle Martini & Rossi extra dry vermouth
2 cups cranberry juice cocktail
1/2 cup Hennessy cognac
1/2 cup sugar
2 oranges, halved and thinly sliced
1 lemon, halved and thinly sliced
2 cups chilled sparkling water

Combine Martini & Rossi extra dry vermouth, cranberry juice, cognac, and sugar in a large pitcher; stir until sugar is dissolved. Chill until ready to serve. Stir in sliced fruit and sparkling water. Serve over ice. Makes 8 1/3 cups.

ULTIMATE IRISH COFFEE

1 1/2 oz. Irish Mist
hot coffee

Topped with whipped cream. No sugar needed.

ULTIMATE MARTINI

3 oz. Bombay Sapphire gin
1 oz. Martini & Rossi extra dry vermouth
1-2 dashes orange bitters (or orange peel)

*Garnish with one cocktail olive and a twist of lemon.
Shake or stir. Serve in a classic martini glass.*

ULTIMATE PUCKER

1 part DeKuyper Pucker watermelon
1 part DeKuyper Pucker sour apple

Chill; serve as a shot.

ULTIMATE TEA

1 1/2 oz. Irish Mist
3 oz. hot tea
bit of lemon

Serve in a mug.

ULTIMATE VOX VODKA MARTINI

1 oz. Vox vodka
1/2 oz. Campari
1/4 oz. Martini & Rossi Rosso vermouth

Shake with ice; strain into a chilled martini glass.

URBAN COCKTAIL

1 oz. Vox vodka
3/4 oz. Hypnotiq
1/4 oz. Bacardi light rum
splash Cointreau
splash Citris

Metrodome
New York City, NY

UTOPIA: IN THE GRANITA STYLE

1/2 glass blueberries, raspberries, and strawberries
2 tsps. fine sugar
3/4 oz. Chambord
champagne

Shake. Champagne to top.

VANILLA APPLES

1 1/4 oz. DeKuyper Pucker sour apple
3/4 oz. DeKuyper Thrilla Vanilla
1/2 oz. Rose's grenadine
2 oz. sweet & sour mix

Top with orange juice. Serve in a tall glass with ice.

VANILLA RILLA

3/4 oz. Bacardi Vaníl
3/4 oz. Bacardi Razz
5 oz. cranberry juice

Pour ingredients over ice. Stir. Serve in a tall glass.

VANILA ROSE

1 oz. Bacardi Vaníl
1/2 oz. DeKuyper wild strawberry liqueur
splash Rose's grenadine
1 1/2 oz. cream

Serve in a rocks glass on ice. Garnish with a maraschino cherry.

Luzi Galvan
Lalo's
Chicago, IL

VICIOUS SID

1 1/2 oz. Bacardi light rum
1/2 oz. Southern Comfort
1/2 oz. Cointreau
1 oz. lemon juice
dash bitters

Shake ingredients with ice and serve over ice.

VOO-DOO DOLL MARTINI

1 1/2 oz. Bacardi Razz
1/2 oz. Chambord
1 oz. cranberry juice
splash sweet & sour mix

Garnish with fresh strawberries.

Belin Jackson
Blue Bayou
Chicago, IL

VOX AND TONIC

2 oz. Vox vodka
3 oz. tonic

*Pour Vox vodka over ice in a tall glass. Fill with tonic.
Add a squeeze of lime.*

VOX BRAVO

....

1/2 oz. Vox vodka
1/2 oz. Campari

Pour Vox vodka and Campari over ice in a tall glass. Top with tonic. Garnish with a slice of lemon and a slice of lime.

VOX COLLINS

....

2 oz. Vox vodka
3/4 oz. sweetened lemon mix
club soda

Shake with ice and pour in a tall glass with ice. Fill with club soda.

VOX GIMLET

....

2 oz. Vox vodka
1/2 oz. fresh lime juice

Mix vodka and lime juice in a glass with ice. Strain and serve in a cocktail glass. Garnish with a twist of lime.

VOX ISLAND ROCKER

....

3 oz. Vox vodka
1 oz. DeKuyper melon liqueur
3 oz. orange juice

Shake with ice and strain into a martini glass. Garnish with an orange slice.

VOX MADRAS

2 oz. Vox vodka
2 oz. orange juice
2 oz. cranberry juice

In a tall glass with ice, fill with half orange juice, half cranberry juice.

VOX BULL SHOT

1 1/4 oz. Vox vodka
5 oz. beef consommé
5 dashes Worcestershire sauce
1 tsp. lemon juice
pinch celery salt or seed

Mix ingredients with ice in a tall glass. Pepper to taste.

VOX SALT AND PEPPER

1 1/4 oz. Vox vodka

Pour chilled vodka into a salt-rimmed cocktail glass. Garnish with a cucumber spear. Pepper to taste.

VOX SALTY DOG

1 1/2 oz. Vox vodka
3/4 oz. grapefruit juice
1/4 tsp. salt

Coat the rim of a glass with salt. Mix and pour on the rocks.

VOX SCREWDRIVER

Vox vodka
freshly squeezed orange juice

Mix over ice in a tall glass.

VOX SEABREEZE

1 1/4 oz. Vox vodka
2 oz. cranberry juice
2 oz. grapefruit juice

Pour vodka over ice in a tall glass. Fill half way with grapefruit juice and top it off with cranberry juice.

VOX VODKA MARTINI

1 1/2 oz. Vox vodka
dash Martini & Rossi extra dry vermouth

Stir. Strain and serve straight up or on the rocks with some ice in a cocktail glass. Add a lemon twist or olive.

VOX WHITE BERRY

3 oz. Vox vodka
1 oz. Cointreau
splash fresh lime juice

Shake with ice; strain into a martini glass. Garnish with a raspberry.

VOX WHITE RUSSIAN

1 oz. Vox vodka
1/2 oz. chocolate liqueur
heavy cream

Pour vodka, chocolate liqueur, and cream over ice in a rocks glass. Shake and serve.

WARD EIGHT

1 1/4 oz. Knob Creek bourbon
4 dashes Rose's grenadine
juice of 1/2 lemon

*Shake ingredients with cracked ice and strain into a glass
with finely cracked ice.*

WARDEN MARTINI

1 1/2 oz. Bombay Sapphire gin
dash Martini & Rossi extra dry vermouth
dash Pernod

*Stir in cocktail glass. Strain and serve straight up or on
the rocks. Add lemon twist or olives.*

WASHINGTON APPLE

2 parts Knob Creek bourbon
1 part DeKuyper Pucker sour apple
2 parts cranberry juice

Serve in a martini glass with a maraschino cherry.

WATERBABY

1 part DeKuyper Pucker watermelon
2 parts pineapple juice

Serve in a tall glass with crushed ice.

WATERMELON AND STRAWBERRY MARGARITA

1 1/2 parts Jose Cuervo Especial
3 parts Jose Cuervo margarita mix
1 1/2 cups (packed) frozen, chopped, and seeded
    watermelon
1/2 cup (packed) frozen, quartered, and unsweetened
    strawberries
1/2 tbs. sugar
pinch salt
watermelon wedge

Puree all ingredients (except watermelon wedge) in a blender until smooth. Pour into a chilled margarita glass. Garnish with a watermelon wedge.

WATERMELON FIZZ

2 parts DeKuyper Pucker watermelon

Fill a glass with lemon-lime soda. Serve over ice in a tall glass.

WATERMELON MARTINI

2 cups cubed watermelon
2 parts Vox vodka
1/4 part sugar syrup
1/2 part DeKuyper Pucker watermelon

Muddle watermelon in base of shaker, add other ingredients; shake with ice and strain into a glass.

WATER MELONTINI

1 part DeKuyper Pucker watermelon
1 part Vox vodka

Garnish with a watermelon slice.

WAVE BREAKER

3/4 oz. Vox vodka
1/2 oz. Cointreau
1/8 oz. lime juice
3/4 oz. Coco Lopez cream of coconut

Blend with ice and strain.

WEEKEND AT THE BEACH

1 oz. DeKuyper Pucker sour apple
1 oz. DeKuyper Peachtree schnapps
2 oz. pineapple juice
2 oz. cranberry juice

Shake with ice. Serve straight up or over ice.

WET KISS

1 part DeKuyper Pucker watermelon
1/2 part Disaronno amaretto
splash lemon

Chill and serve as a shot.

WHISKEY SOUR

1 1/2 oz. Knob Creek bourbon
3/4 oz. sweetened lemon juice
1 tsp. superfine sugar

Shake with ice. Serve straight up or over ice.

WHISPER

1/2 oz. Martini & Rossi dry vermouth
grated lime or lemon peel
1 oz. Vox vodka
1 oz. Cointreau

Pour dry vermouth, vodka, and Cointreau into a mixing glass with ice. Stir. Strain into a cocktail glass.

WHISPER MARTINI

1 1/2 oz. Vox vodka
1 or 2 drops Martini & Rossi dry vermouth

Garnish to taste.

WHITE LADY

2 parts Bombay Sapphire gin
1 part Cointreau
1 part sweetened lemon mix

Shake well with ice and serve on the rocks.

WHITE RUSSIAN

Pour 1 1/2 parts DeKuyper coffee liqueur and 1 part Vox vodka over ice. Top with 1 1/2 parts cream. Shake with ice. Serve straight up or on ice.

WIDOW MAKER

1/2 oz. Drambuie
1 oz. Knob Creek bourbon
1/2 oz. Dewar's scotch
1 oz. lemon juice
1 oz. orange juice

In an old-fashioned glass, shake with ice, strain over ice.

WILD IRISH ROSE

1 1/2 oz. Tullamore Dew Irish whiskey
1 1/2 tsp. Rose's grenadine
1/2 oz. Rose's lime juice
club soda

Fill a highball glass with ice. Add Tullamore Dew Irish whiskey, grenadine, and lime juice. Stir well. Fill with club soda.

WILD ROVER

1 part Carolans Irish cream
1 part Irish Mist

Serve on the rocks.

WINTER WARM-UP

2 oz. Chambord
1/2 oz. DeKuyper coffee liqueur
3 oz. hot coffee
whipped cream

Serve in a coffee cup or mug.

WOLF HOUND

1 oz. Tullamore Dew Irish whiskey
3/4 oz. DeKuyper dark crème de cacao
1/2 oz. half-and-half
splash club soda

Stir ingredients with ice and serve over ice.

WOO WOO

3/4 oz. Vox vodka
3/4 oz. DeKuyper peppermint schnapps

Shake with ice. Serve in a shot glass or over ice.

WOODY MELON

2 shots DeKuyper Pucker watermelon
1/2 shot Knob Creek bourbon
squeeze of lemon

Shake and serve over ice.

YELLOW BIRD

3/4 oz. Bacardi rum
1/4 oz. Liquore Galliano
1/4 oz. DeKuyper crème de banana
2 oz. pineapple juice
2 oz. orange juice

Shake. Serve in a tall glass.

YELLOW FELLOW

1 oz. Bombay Sapphire gin
1/4 oz. yellow Chartreuse

Shake. Strain into a cocktail glass.

YUCATAN MARGARITA WITH TROPICAL FRUIT

1 1/2 parts Jose Cuervo Especial
3 parts Jose Cuervo margarita mix
1 tbs. papaya nectar
1 tbs. guava nectar
1 tbs. cream of coconut
lime slice
lime wedge
sugar

Rub rim of margarita glass with a lime wedge. Dip rim into sugar. Combine Jose Cuervo Especial, Jose Cuervo margarita mix, papaya nectar, guava nectar, cream of coconut, and ice in a mixing glass. Shake well. Pour into a margarita glass. Garnish with a lime slice.

ZOMBIE

3/4 oz. Bacardi light rum
1/4 oz. Bacardi dark rum
1/4 tsp. Bacardi 151 rum
1 oz. pineapple juice
1 oz. orange juice
1 oz. lemon or Rose's lime juice

Mix the first two rums and all juices with ice in a shaker or blender and pour into a tall glass. Float 1/4 tsp. Bacardi 151, garnish with a pineapple spear and a maraschino cherry.

NONALCOHOLIC DRINKS

BANANA LOPEZ

2 oz. Coco Lopez cream of coconut
1 med. banana
1 tsp. lemon juice
1 cup ice

Mix in a blender until smooth.

COCO LOPEZ SHAKE

2 1/2 oz. Coco Lopez cream of coconut
1 scoop vanilla ice cream
1 cup ice

Mix in a blender until smooth.

DUST CUTTER

3/4 oz. Rose's lime juice
6 oz. Schweppes tonic water

Combine over ice in a tall glass.

FLORIDA BANANA LOPEZ

2 oz. Coco Lopez cream of coconut
4 oz. orange juice
1 med. banana
1 cup ice

Mix in a blender until smooth.

GRAPE LOPEZ

3 oz. Coco Lopez cream of coconut
4 oz. grape juice
1 1/2 cups ice

Mix in a blender until smooth.

NADA COLADA

1 oz. Coco Lopez cream of coconut
2 oz. pineapple juice
1 cup ice

Mix in a blender until smooth.

ORANGE SMOOTHIE

2 1/2 oz. Coco Lopez cream of coconut
3 oz. orange juice
1 scoop vanilla ice cream
1 cup ice
nutmeg

Mix in a blender until smooth. Sprinkle with nutmeg.

ORANGE SORBET LOPEZ

2 oz. Coco Lopez cream of coconut
1 oz. orange juice
1 scoop orange sherbet
1/2 cup ice

Mix in a blender until smooth.

RUBY COOLER

1 cup Ocean Spray cranapple juice
1 tsp. instant tea
lemon wedges

Mix together cranapple juice and tea. Pour over ice into two tall glasses with lemon wedge garnishes.

SHIRLEY TEMPLE

1 oz. Rose's grenadine
5 oz. ginger ale

Pour ingredients over ice in a tall glass. Garnish with a maraschino cherry.

STRAWBERRY BANANA LOPEZ

2 oz. Coco Lopez cream of coconut
2 oz. strawberries
1/2 med. banana
1 cup ice

Mix in a blender until smooth.

VIRGIN MARY

4 oz. tomato juice
dash Worcestershire sauce
dash Tabasco sauce
dash salt and pepper
dash celery salt
dash soy sauce

In a glass filled with ice, add tomato juice. Add a dash or two of Worcestershire sauce, Tabasco, salt, and pepper. Garnish with a celery stalk.

INDEX

ABOUT THE AUTHOR

Jaclyn Wilson Foley has been the editor of *Bartender* magazine for over twenty years. She resides in Liberty Corner, New Jersey, with her husband and partner, Ray Foley, founder of *Bartender* magazine.